A NEW CHAPTER

IN THE

EARLY LIFE OF WASHINGTON,

IN CONNECTION WITH THE

NARRATIVE HISTORY

OF THE

POTOMAC COMPANY.

BY

JOHN PICKELL.

NEW YORK:
D. APPLETON & CO., 346 AND 348 BROADWAY.
1856.

PHILADELPHIA:

T. K. AND P. G. COLLINS, PRINTERS.

DEDICATION.

TO THE HONORABLE JOHN P. KENNEDY.

MY DEAR SIR:—

In 1823, after the lapse of many years, the project of connecting the East and the West, through the valleys of the Potomac River, and that of the most convenient tributary to the Ohio west of the mountains, was revived in the form of a proposition for a continuous canal navigation. To consummate this connection, required the rights and privileges secured under the existing charter of the Potomac Company to be surrendered. This was done; the Chesapeake and Ohio Canal Company was organized, and all the original papers, books, records, and notes, belonging to that *time-honored* enterprise, were deposited in its office.

My connection with this Company for several years, as one of the Board of Directors, enabled me to collect the interesting details for the narrative from the materials thus deposited. Their arrangement in chronological order required much care and labor, but was necessary to give it the unity of history. To preserve it in this form I was not altogether prompted by motives of personal interest; it appeared to me a duty to avail myself of the opportunity that was afforded, to give the authenticated facts to the public, however unimportant in themselves, in which the FATHER OF HIS COUNTRY took the most prominent part, and which might contribute to shed additional light upon the beauty, the harmony, and the virtue of his illustrious life.

The extracts from the private correspondence of General Washington, and for which I am indebted to the kindness of Mr. Jared Sparks, form perhaps the most interesting part of the volume.

In appropriating my labors, I cannot refrain from their introduction to the American public, through the name of one whose public and private life is distinguished by every virtue that adorns the good citizen, the patriotic legislator, and the sound statesman. Recognizing in him also a highly valued personal friend, I felt that I could not manifest my appreciation of that friendship more suitably than by the dedication of the volume which adds a new item to the history of the life of the *greatest* and *best*.

I am, most respectfully,

Your obedient servant,

THE AUTHOR.

INTRODUCTORY REMARKS.

The conspicuous part it was the glory of WASHINGTON to act upon the theatre of public affairs, during one of the most eventful periods in the history of the world; the universal dignity and charm of his demeanor in all the relations of life in which he was placed; the affability and disinterested kindness of his intercourse with others; the virtuous simplicity of his retirement after the consummation of his country's independence; the harmony of his public and his private life; the purity of his patriotism and the splendor of his military career, formed altogether such a union of goodness and greatness in the character of one individual as was calculated to excite the warmest interest, and command the admiration of mankind.

An accomplished classical writer, in his portraiture of this illustrious personage, truly and eloquently says: "He united the intrepidity of Aristides, the patriotism of Cato, the military prudence of Cæsar, and the humanity of Scipio. He was to his own beloved country, what Themistocles and Solon were to the Grecian States; and what Numa and Camillus were to the Roman Commonwealth."

He was great and good in all the positions he occupied.

We trace him first as a simple member of a surveying party, among the wilds and glades of the Alleghany Mountains—then as the special messenger from the Colonial Governor of Virginia, to the French commandant on the Ohio—next at the memorable military defence of the stockade at the Great Meadows—then at the head of his regiment upon the bloody plains of the Monongahela—as a member of the House of Burgesses—as a delegate to the first Congress, in 1774—as the Commander-in-Chief of the Army of the Revolution—at Annapolis resigning his sword and his commission into the hands of the representatives of the nation—afterwards as President of the POTOMAC COMPANY—and finally as Chief Magistrate of the Union; and closes his career in beautiful and simple retirement.

Is it then a matter of surprise that there should cluster around the memory of this illustrious man, the warmest affections of the American people; the deepest veneration of every friend of mankind?

In the beautiful and appropriate language of Matthew Henry, "the remains of good and great men, like the mantle of Elijah, ought to be gathered up and preserved by successive generations; their sayings, their writings, their doings; their examples;

that, as their works follow them, when they are gone, these stay behind to benefit mankind, and are their reward."

Recognizing the force and propriety of these sentiments, the compiler of the following pages must congratulate himself that an opportunity was afforded to him to rescue from oblivion a chapter in the life of a man that so honored humanity, and to gather up in a form to be perpetuated, the sayings, writings, doings, and example, with which that chapter is connected.

However unimportant the facts may be in themselves, they are not the less calculated to keep alive, in the affections of generations to come, the memory of him who was "first in war, first in peace, and first in the hearts of his countrymen." Let us be persuaded that while his memory is suitably revered, the integrity of the Union will be secured, and the blessings of civil and religious liberty enjoyed in our country.

The extensive correspondence in which WASHINGTON was engaged after the close of the Revolutionary War, with the leading men of the country, relative to the great subject of Internal Improvement, is highly interesting, and is in fact an important item of history. This correspondence shows that he felt more than an ordinary solicitude about the establishment of a scheme of strengthening the bonds of union by means of internal communication.

A strong feeling was early awakened in favor of the specific plan he set on foot, among the public-spirited men of Virginia and Maryland, even before the rupture with the mother country; and after the close of that memorable struggle, it assumed a more general character, and was emphatically impressed upon the public consideration as a measure of national policy.

The original history of the POTOMAC COMPANY is the nucleus around which the contents of this monograph are put together; and the narrative corresponds almost literally with the record of proceedings of that company. The connection of the compiler with the CHESAPEAKE AND OHIO CANAL COMPANY for several years, enabled him to have access to the books and papers that were deposited in the office, in 1828, when its charter was surrendered. The books and papers were collated and examined with much care, and disposed in their proper chronological order. This was a work of labor, and as it is the groundwork of this volume, no pains were spared to make it as complete as possible.

The particular interest which attaches to these parts of the compilation flows from the fact, that the proceedings recorded were originally drawn up either by Washington himself, as the first President of the company, or examined and reviewed by him before they were transferred to the books, and that in all the histories that have been written of his life, not one, as far as the knowledge of the compiler has extended, gives any details in reference to his connection with this enterprise, and of which he was the chosen head from its organization, in 1784, to his retirement, in 1788.

The material facts and circumstances embraced in the part of the volume which precedes the narrative of the POTOMAC COMPANY, and with which WASHINGTON was connected, were generally obtained by the most diligent and laborious examinations, from such numbers of the Colonial Gazettes and publications of the earliest date, as the compiler could get access to.

For the extracts, in the third part of the volume, relative to the POTOMAC COMPANY, and to the policy of internal communication, the compiler is indebted to the kindness of Mr. Jared Sparks, who generously granted him the privilege of using his valuable collection of the writings of WASHINGTON. These interesting extracts present in a clear and distinct view the sentiments and opinions entertained by the illustrious originator of the measure of public policy to which they refer, and will without doubt greatly engage the attention of the reader.

PART I.

A NUMBER of years anterior to the commencement of the Revolutionary War, the project of uniting the two great divisions of the country, separated by the Alleghany range of mountains, by means of a public highway, was entertained by some of the most prominent and distinguished individuals of Virginia and Maryland.

In the latter part of the year 1753 Major Washington, then only 21 years of age, was delegated by the Governor and Council of Virginia on an important mission across the Alleghanies. Having been actively engaged during the greater part of the three years immediately preceding his appointment in surveying the wild lands of Western Virginia and in the mountainous district at the head-waters of the Potomac River; and already possessing a deservedly high character for energy, firmness and decision; with a thorough knowledge of the peculiar feelings and prejudices of the Indians; a practical acquaintance with

2

the mode of living and travelling, and withal accustomed to the privations, hardships and exposure of a camp life in a wilderness country, the attention of Governor Dinwiddie was readily attracted to him, as the individual who combined in the greatest degree the qualifications suited to the discharge of the delicate and responsible duties of the mission. He was accordingly selected. His commission (Appendix A), the letter of instructions (B), and passport (C) were prepared with much care, and formally presented to him by the Governor at the seat of government on the 30th day of October, 1753.

Immediately after the presentation of the credentials, he took his departure from Williamsburg amid the warm congratulations and good wishes of the Colonial Government and numerous friends who had called upon him on the occasion. He first proceeded to Alexandria, where he remained several days occupied in making the necessary arrangements for the journey, and then proceeded on his mission to the valley of the Ohio by the way of Wills' Creek. After a tedious and laborious journey of nearly three weeks, he reached his destination; and, in pursuance of the letter of his instructions, continued there no longer than was absolutely necessary to the faithful discharge of the important duties devolving upon him under the authority of his *special* commission. On his return, he directed his course to a more southern route, and entered the valley of the Potomac, not far north of the sources of the Shenandoah River.

Notwithstanding the inclement season of the year when the journeys were performed, he took daily notes of the incidents as he proceeded, and sketched, with remarkable precision and graphic power, the physical features and topography of the country through which he travelled. On his return to Williamsburg, he made a verbal report of the result of the mission to the Governor and members of the Council, and presented to them the manuscript journal of his travels across the mountains.

From the imperfect record that is left of his personal interview with Governor Dinwiddie, it is fair to infer that he availed himself of the occasion to suggest the importance of opening a communication, by means of a public road, between the settlements east and west of the mountains. The suggestion, however, does not owe its origin so much to the consideration of facilitating trade and social intercourse between these two parts of the country, as to the idea of affording military protection to the remote settlements, and a defence against the aggressions of the French and their Indian allies upon the territory claimed by the British crown.

Previous to the mission of Major Washington, the West was known only as a dense and extensive wilderness; traversed by watercourses and rivers; broken by lofty mountains and deep valleys, and inhabited by wandering and warlike tribes of Indians. Few of the prominent citizens of the Atlantic colonies at this period had an adequate idea of the character of the mountainous belt of country which intervened between the westernmost settlements of the eastern declivity of the Alleghany range and the western waters; and no disposition was manifested to explore it, at the expense of the enjoyments and comforts of their homes, and at the imminent peril of their lives. Huntsmen, trappers and Indian traders were occasionally seen wending their way through its dark valleys, and over their rough and rocky acclivities; but these laborious and dangerous journeys were not undertaken to acquire personal knowledge of the country with a view to its occupation or improvement. The object was gain by the toilsome prosecution of the particular pursuit in which these adventurers were engaged; and they were rather more inclined to magnify the difficulties they encountered in traversing the country in quest of hunting and trading grounds, than to give a candid representation of the character of the soil; of the broad and beautiful valleys and noble streams they had so often beheld beyond the mountains.

Under these circumstances, it was fortunate for the country that an occasion occurred which called into active requisition the services of the youthful Washington, an occasion that opened the bud which in after years developed to maturity, in the perfect greatness of the "Father of his Country." By the energy, the industry, and the fearlessness he manifested in the progress of his journey through an almost untrodden wilderness of several hundred miles in extent, and the intelligence and sagacity and judgment displayed in the management of the affairs of the mission, he drew around him the unqualified confidence and esteem of the authorities of Virginia. On his return, he was immediately complimented by a military promotion to the grade of Lieut. Colonel of the regular forces, and in that capacity joined the brave, but ill-fated Braddock, and his army in the following year at the junction of the Youghiogheny and Monongahela rivers a few days before the disastrous battle.

Notwithstanding the entire defeat of the army under General Braddock, there were displays of military skill and courage on the part of the officers and men which embalm their names in our grateful recollection, and adorn that otherwise dark page of American history with peculiar brightness. Among the most conspicuous, Colonel Washington stood preeminent. The House of Burgesses, which convened at Williamsburg in August following, unanimously passed a vote of thanks to Col. Washington and his officers "for their bravery and gallant defence of their country." All the proceedings of the campaign were approved and applauded by the people, and Washington, thus cheered and encouraged in his patriotic efforts to serve his country, his determination to retire from the army was for a time delayed, and the chain of events which connected him with the subsequent history of the country remained unbroken.

In a letter which he wrote to his brother a few days after the battle, dated Fort Cumberland (D), July 18th, he says: "By the all-powerful dispensations of Providence, I have been protected beyond all human probability or expectation; for I had four bullets through my coat, and two horses shot under me, yet escaped unhurt, although death was levelling my companions on every side of me."

The Reverend Samuel Daviess, subsequently President of the college at Princeton, on the 17th day of August delivered an address, which both by its title and tenor is so remarkably characteristic of the times, and so prophetic, that I cannot deem it entirely out of place to refer to it, and introduce a brief extract from it. "Religion and Patriotism, the Constituents of a Good Soldier," was its appropriate title. The knowledge of the defeat of Braddock and his army created much alarm, and aroused a military spirit in the country of the most effective character. Volunteer companies were organized in almost all the colonies, and the sound of preparation to march to the frontiers for the protection of the settlements was heard in every direction. Forces from the north, south, and middle colonies were ready to unite and place themselves under the command of the gallant chief whose military achievements at the Great Meadows (E) and upon the bloody plains of the Monongahela had already won for him the title of a "hero."

The reverend speaker, after applauding this noble spirit which pervaded the country, in terms of the highest pride and satisfaction, paused for a moment, and then, as if moved by inspiration, continued: "I may point out to the public that heroic youth, Colonel Washington, whom I cannot but hope Providence has hitherto preserved in so signal a manner for some important service to his country."

Colonel Washington continued in the military service of the colony until the termination of the campaign in 1758, when he resigned his commission, and in the following year was elected a member of the House of Burgesses.

An interesting circumstance is related in Wirt's "Life of Patrick Henry," illustrative of the modesty of the distinguished youth, who, for the first time, was introduced to a legislative body as one of its members, and is so characteristic of true merit, that I trust its insertion here needs no apology.

"A short time after Col. Washington had taken his seat, the speaker, Mr. John Robinson, in obedience to an order of the House, rose, and in an eloquent and impressive manner, tendered to him the thanks of the House for his eminent public services, and expatiated in language of the highest admiration upon his military achievements, and the importance of the services he had rendered the country." When

Washington rose to express his grateful sense of the honor they had conferred upon him, in noticing his public services in this distinguished manner, the biographer remarks: "He hesitated, stammered, and trembled, and was so much confused that he stood hesitating for a few moments, when the speaker relieved him by a stroke of address that would have done honor to Louis XIV. in his proudest and happiest moment, and said, with a conciliating smile: 'Sit down, Mr. Washington; your modesty is equal to your valor, and that surpasses the power of any language that I possess.'"

There is no evidence in the recorded proceedings of the House of Burgesses of this session, that the subject of opening a communication with the West was introduced. The scheme he had originally indicated to Governor Dinwiddie was not, however, abandoned; it continued to be cherished by him with undiminished favor. In his personal intercourse with the members, he took occasion to commend the project as worthy of their favorable consideration; and he determined, before it should be formally brought before the legislature of the colony for its definite action, to supply himself with such facts as would show the feasibility of the project, the expense of its construction, and the advantages that would flow from the proposed improvement.

For this purpose, mainly, he made several tours of examination to the sources of the Potomac River and the country intervening, to the navigable points of the western waters, in the years 1770, 1772, and 1774. The selection of the best route was of the first importance, and to this object his personal efforts were particularly directed.

Few of the large streams issuing directly from the eastern and western slopes of the Appalachian chain were known at this early period, beyond the line of settlements. Their sources were either conjectured, or located upon vague and indefinite information, derived generally from hunters and trappers; or from those whose erratic wanderings from their temporary habitations in the plains and depths of ravines and valleys, not unfrequently led them to the heads of the streams or opposite sides of the mountains, and enabled them to form estimates, with tolerable accuracy, of the distances across the portage. Well defined Indian and traders' paths, connecting these points, intersected each other at various angles, and greatly facilitated the explorations of the summit range. Several surveying parties were for some time engaged at different points, running lines and marking boundaries; and in collecting materials for a map, and an analysis of the middle colonies. Captain Thomas Hutchins, a bold, intrepid and intelligent woodsman, led the advance in this arduous and dangerous service. The surveys and explorations of these parties were noted with remarkable correctness. The topographical description of Western Virginia, and Maryland especially, exhibits interesting details of the entire surface of the eastern and western slopes and summits of the mountain range between the State lines of Pennsylvania and North Carolina.

The maps that were plotted of the several surveys made by these parties, were critically examined by Colonel Washington, and materially aided him in selecting the most feasible route for the contemplated communication between the Atlantic colonies and the Western Territory.

Naturally fearless in the pursuit of a patriotic object, he allowed no difficulties or dangers to check him in the progress of his searches among the gorges and fastnesses of the formidable barrier which interposed, in the accomplishment of his favorite scheme. He penetrated to the very fountain sources—made laborious reconnoissances of the intervening summits—strictly scrutinized all the advantages and disadvantages of their ground, and took ample notes of the diversified features of the country, within the range of the examination—thus preparing himself with the most important facts, to sustain the proposition upon its presentation to the legislatures of the colonies more immediately interested.

In his letter to Mr. Jefferson, dated in 1784, ten years after his last tour across the mountains, in reference to the route, and the policy of opening the communication, he says: "I have, I think, clearly pointed out the advantages of the route I have selected, and the wisdom of the policy on the part of the States (Virginia and Maryland), to render it facile."

The territories of Virginia and Maryland, being divided by the Potomac, made it the interest of these two colonies to be proportionably concerned in the improvement of its navigation, and the extension of the communication by a public highway to the valley of the Ohio. It was evident that the western trade would soon be a matter of importance, and could only be secured to those points on the Atlantic side to which the earliest and most improved channel would be opened. The sagacious and observant mind of Washington foresaw clearly that the great western region would rapidly be peopled by an energetic and industrious population; that its valleys and its plains would be checkered with cultivated fields, and meadows, and villages; that its numerous navigable streams would be active channels of trade and internal commerce, and that the multifarious interests of enlightened and prosperous communities would soon extend their beneficent influences over the wide valleys of the Ohio River and its tributaries; and that a wise and just policy prompted the earliest adoption of the measure he proposed to bring before the legislatures of the respective colonies.

It was the invariable custom of Washington, from the age of eighteen years, to take notes of the most important circumstances and events in which he was personally concerned; and whilst travelling, to keep a daily journal of the incidents as they occurred in the progress of his journey. In this journal he particularly noticed the peculiarities and fertility of the soil, and the natural growth of the country through which he passed, to which were added such reflections and considerations as the occasion would suggest to a mind equally imbued with the power of close observation and deep thought. This custom had acquired with him the force of habit, and rendered his observations both highly interesting and instructive.

Shortly after his return from the western tour, in 1770, a portion of his journal and extracts from his letters, to some of his friends in Virginia and Maryland, were published in several of the Colonial Gazettes, and were widely circulated and read. As was naturally to be expected, from the character of these papers, their perusal awakened a spirit of inquiry, and with it a strong desire among the energetic and enterprising of the youthful population to emigrate to the west, and in a few years hundreds of that class of the population of the Atlantic colonies had emigrated thither.

When Washington made his next tour, in 1774, he was surprised at the change that had already taken place in the valley of the Ohio River. With a mind that could clearly anticipate the future, he beheld, at no distant day, that remote wilderness of the great and extensive West the abode of dense and enterprising communities; in the possession and enjoyment of all the elements of social and political prosperity; and, to hasten this consummation, he regarded the opening of a communication by a public highway between the East and the West as of the first importance.

Entertaining these views, he brought the subject before the House of Burgesses, at its regular session, in 1774, and urged it earnestly upon the attention of the members, as a measure of public policy. But striving, for a long time in vain, for aid from the colony, he was compelled to change his original design; and he introduced and moved the adoption of a bill to empower individuals to subscribe to the enterprise, and accomplish the improvement on certain expressed conditions, at their own expense. Even with this essential modification, the project was opposed—the largest share of the opposition coming from Central Virginia. To allay the hostility from this populous part of the colony, an amendment was incorporated in the bill to include in its provisions the improvement of the navigation of James River. This measure of compromise seemed to reconcile the conflicting sectional interests of the colony; and, had time allowed, would have secured a passage of the bill in the House of Burgesses.

But the prospects of a similar bill before the General Assembly of Maryland were not so encouraging.

To give availability to any enactment, the concurrent action of the legislatures of the two colonies was necessary, so far, at least, as regarded the improvement of the channel of the Potomac River. Jealousies, and the rivalries for the western trade, had already grown up between the citizens of Georgetown and the merchants of Baltimore; and whatever efforts for aid were made by one party in the legislature, were counteracted by the other. Applications, memorials, protests, and remonstrances, followed each other in quick succession, and the friends and advocates of the scheme despaired of success during the pending session.

This was the doubtful condition of the favorite project of Washington, and to which the earliest energies of his mind had been steadily directed, when he was called, by his appointment (F) of Commander-in-Chief of the Army in 1775, to Cambridge. The war which immediately followed the affair at Lexington, in April of this year, drew the public mind to more engrossing objects; and during the continuance of that memorable struggle for national existence and independence, and until the retirement of the illustrious chief in 1783, the prosecution of this measure was entirely suspended.

The indications, however, in the House of Burgesses at the commencement of the Revolutionary War, were sufficiently favorable to encourage the belief that, in the event of the successful termination of that contest, no further difficulty would be experienced in obtaining from that body at a subsequent session all the powers and privileges that were embraced in the bill of 1774, and which were considered entirely adequate to carry into operation the original views and intentions of the friends of the project.

In Maryland, the prospect of eventual success was not so flattering. The union of the merchants of Baltimore, an enterprising, intelligent, and wealthy community, exercised a controlling influence, not only over the deliberations and actions of the General Assembly, but moulded public sentiment in opposition to any measure which was supposed would divert any of its trade to another market; and precluded the hope that any future session would in the least abate its hostility to a proposition of this character, or which did not directly or indirectly promote its business and commercial prosperity.

PART II.

In 1783, the war of the Revolution terminated by a treaty which recognized and acknowledged the independence of the United States. Soon after that memorable event, the illustrious Washington resigned his commission (G) of commander-in-chief of the army into the hands of Congress at Annapolis, and immediately thereafter proceeded to Mount Vernon, where, as he beautifully and feelingly expresses it, "he hoped to spend the remainder of his days, in cultivating the affections of good men, and in the practice of the domestic virtues."

Here, in his favorite retreat, secluded from the cares and anxieties of public life, crowned with glory and with honor, the beloved Washington cherished the hope of continuing in the enjoyment of that tranquillity and freedom from official responsibilities and cares which years of long public service had made particularly desirable.

Notwithstanding the agreeableness of this retirement, he did not abandon the favorite enterprise of his early years (H). Contemplating from its quiet shades the wide extent of country which had risen from a condition of colonial dependence to a confederation of sovereign States, he was the more impressed with the importance of the measure as a matter of national concern, of the wisdom of the policy of connecting the East and the West by a public highway, and of the adoption of a *system* of internal improvement, of which this proposed communication was to be the introduction. Fully persuaded of the propriety of his views, he opened an extensive correspondence on the subject with some of the most distinguished sages and patriots of the "times that tried the souls of men." He advocated the policy upon the broad, patriotic, and lofty principle of a common interest, or, in other words, of the *general welfare;* and although General Washington cherished full confidence in the stability of the popular institutions of the government, and in the inviolability of the UNION, yet, with a wisdom and a forethought at that early period of our experience peculiarly his own, he regarded the facilitation of social intercourse between the populations of the extreme parts of our broad and extended territory, and the mutual interchange of trade and commerce by means of public roads and highways, as important auxiliaries in binding still more closely the sovereignties of the States in one fraternal, indissoluble compact.

The enterprise of the POTOMAC COMPANY was well calculated, in his view, to take the lead in this patriotic scheme. It was considered feasible, and at a comparatively moderate cost. The route he had suggested embraced a wider range of interests than any other that could at that time be proposed to connect the East with the West, the Atlantic markets with the fields of production, the purchasers and consumers with the producers.

The condition of the country under the confederative government rendered the policy of establishing a judicious system of national internal improvement obviously apparent. The vast extent of the public domain in the *far west*, and in several of the States; the importance of facilitating the transportation of the mails; the establishment of post-offices, and encouragements to the settlement of the public lands, were among the principal considerations which imposed upon the government the imperative duty to aid and foster the system, in the infancy of the existence of the republic. And these considerations did not fail to be fully appreciated by the FATHER OF HIS COUNTRY.

Having enjoyed the quietude of his retirement for a few months, he left Mount Vernon on his first tour to the West after the close of the Revolutionary War, on the first day of September, 1784. The principal objects in view were to examine the condition of his lands in that country; to renew his recollection of the features of the dividing ridge he had formerly examined, and to extend his observations beyond the limits to which they were originally confined. He proceeded directly to Fort Cumberland, where he remained a few days to prepare for the journey. A great extent of wilderness and mountain district lay before him, and through which it was not only necessary for him to travel, but, in order to carry out the intentions which mainly prompted the journey, to make an extensive and critical reconnoissance of the summit range which intervened between the head-waters of the Potomac and the Ohio Rivers. This was not an easy service; it was one of toil and peril. When General Washington reached the first settlement beyond Fort Cumberland, he was advised of the great dissatisfaction which prevailed among the Indians inhabiting the country at the sources of the Cheat, Youghiogheny, Monongahela, and Savage Rivers; and was cautioned not unnecessarily to expose himself to their wiles and treachery, while he would be engaged in the examinations.

This information did not deter him from his original purpose, nor in the least abate his zeal in the pursuit of his patriotic object. He devoted several weeks to the arduous duties he had assumed, and supplied himself with facts and arguments of the most convincing character relative to the route he had selected for the proposed communication. His plan contemplated the improvement of the navigation of the Potomac from tide-water to the mouth of Wills' Creek, or to the highest practicable point of the Potomac, and connect it by a road or highway across the portage with the navigable waters of the Cheat, the Youghiogheny, and the Monongahela Rivers; or more directly with the Ohio.

After having completed the examination of the several portages across the mountains and of the head-waters of the streams with which he proposed to connect, he returned to Mount Vernon on the 4th day of October, 1784. On his return, he took a more southern route, and entered upon the eastern slope of the dividing ridge near the sources of the Shenandoah River, and descended upon the valley at a point not far from the site of the beautiful and flourishing town of Staunton. The entire distance he travelled during this tour exceeded six hundred and fifty miles. Generally, it was performed on horseback; but in numerous instances, on account of the rough and rocky character of the country, he was compelled to dismount, lead his horse, and travel on foot. With few intervals, the routes that were examined lay through uncultivated, wild, and mountainous districts. Since his first exploration of the country in 1774, the improvement he had suggested as a means merely of defence and protection to the settlements west of the mountains against the hostile aggressions of the French and Indians, had materially changed its character. It had now become a measure of great national importance, both as regarded its effect upon trade and upon the integrity of the confederation, now the UNION OF THE STATES.

Shortly after his return to Mount Vernon, he prepared an interesting report of the proceedings of his tour, and the convictions of his own mind in reference to the object of his journey; which, with a transcript of his journal, he transmitted to the Governor of Virginia. In his report he not only affirms, but clearly demonstrates, the practicability of the project, and recommends it to his favorable consideration with great powers of argument. He forcibly illustrates the advantages of its adoption by an array of facts which are incontrovertible, and presented in the report especially for the consideration of the legislature, as arguments indorsing the wisdom of the measure proposed as a means of strengthening the bonds of union between the East and the West, and, besides, eminently calculated to promote the general prosperity of the States. Upon the desirable results of the adoption of the policy suggested in his report, he dwells with peculiar emphasis and satisfaction. To its accomplishment he had directed his earliest and untiring energies, and now, at a maturer period, commends it as worthy of the countenance and favor of every patriot in the land.

Entertaining a sincere wish for the success and good name of the administration of his warm personal friend Governor Harrison, he adds to this report the following language: "If you concur with me in the proposition I have suggested, and it is adopted by the legislature, it will signalize your administration as an important era in the history of this country."

On another occasion, not long subsequent to the date of his communication to Governor Harrison, he addressed a letter of similar import to a distinguished member of Congress, in which he recommends the project with equal earnestness and force. As a measure of public policy, he remarks: "There is a matter, which, though it does not come before Congress *wholly*, is in my opinion of great political importance, and ought to be attended to in time. It is to prevent the trade of the western territory from settling into the hands of the Spaniards or the British. But, it may be asked, How are we to prevent this? Happily for us, the way is plain. Extend the navigation of the eastern waters; communicate them as near as possible with those which run westward—open those to the Ohio; open also such as extend from the Ohio towards Lake Erie, and we shall not only draw the produce of the western settlers, but the peltry and the fur trade of the lakes to our ports; thus adding an immense increase to our exports, and binding these people to us by a chain which can never be broken."

These two interesting communications contain the first suggestion and general outline of the system of *internal improvements* which was afterwards adopted by the general government as a favorite measure of national policy (I), and continued to be sustained by Congress until the year 1829, when it was abandoned in consequence of the exercise of the *veto* power of the Executive relative to the bill appropriating a specific amount for constructing the *Maysville road.*

It does not come within the province or design of the compiler, or comport with the nature of this work, to analyze the policy of the system to which he has adverted; or to enter into a critical examination of the local or general effects which have resulted from its adoption by the government. But it may be well, when we are disposed to examine the principle of this measure, as a matter of public policy, to bring into view the vast extent of unoccupied territory which came into the possession of the government upon the achievement of our separate national existence; to investigate the political propriety of affording facilities for its settlement and improvement, and the importance of spreading the already dense population of the sea-board communities. With these prominent considerations before the mind, an adequate conception may be entertained of the extraordinary sagacity, wisdom, and foresight of the illustrious projector, when he originally suggested the particular enterprise of opening an internal communication between the waters of the Atlantic and the Ohio River, and more especially when it is remembered that the suggestion was made long anterior to the separation of the colonies from the dominion of the British crown.

At this early period, and indeed for several years after the adoption of the constitution in 1789, the population comparatively was confined to a narrow strip of country along the Atlantic borders. The almost unbounded territory west of the Appalachian chain was, with few exceptions, an unbroken wilderness, occupied by unknown numbers and tribes of Indians, many of whom were of the most ferocious and savage character. Hence, it was not an easy matter to stimulate the public to engage in enterprises of internal communications. More than the mere knowledge of the present, was necessary to secure the confidence of the people in projects of this nature. The universal respect that was entertained for General Washington; the unqualified confidence in his judgment, and in the wisdom and purity of the purpose which prompted all his actions, were, however, sufficient to enlist the attention of the Legislature of Virginia to entertain the proposition, until it could be brought before them in a more definite form. Accompanied by his distinguished friend and compatriot Marquis de Lafayette, he made a visit to Richmond while the legislature was in session, where he was received with all the love and affection which an enlightened, grateful, and patriotic people could bestow upon the FATHER OF HIS COUNTRY. But with all the honors that were showered upon him by the authorities and every class of his fellow-citizens, in the most unbounded profusion, the favorite enterprise of his youthful days, which time and circumstances had matured into a scheme of national character, was not forgotten or neglected. His letter, previously addressed to Governor Harrison, was communicated to the legislature, and referred to an appropriate committee. In a few days the chairman reported a bill in accordance with its views, which was passed with remarkable unanimity.

Having accomplished the purpose of his visit to Richmond, he returned to Mount Vernon, and from thence immediately addressed a letter to Mr. Madison, then a young but already distinguished member of the Virginia Legislature, on the subject of his recent visit to the seat of government. In this letter, he earnestly recommended (as the concurrent action of Maryland was necessary to render a bill available) the appointment of commissioners, invested with full powers to confer with such gentlemen as might be selected by the Legislature of Maryland, to prepare the form of a bill which in its character and provisions would be acceptable to both States. Mr. Madison at once concurred in the propriety of the recommendation, and immediately moved the appointment of a deputation of three individuals for the purpose of carrying its suggestions into effect; the motion was adopted, and General Washington, General Gates, and Colonel Blackburn were appointed.

The deputation, with the exception of Colonel Blackburn (who was prevented by serious indisposition), proceeded to Annapolis about the 20th day of December, 1784. On their arrival in the ancient metropolis of Maryland, they were received with the most distinguished demonstrations of respect and confidence, and were formally welcomed by the citizens and corporate authorities, and by a committee of the legislature.

General Washington, in behalf of the Virginia deputation, communicated to the General Assembly the object of their visit. A committee was immediately appointed by the legislature, composed of Thomas Stone, Samuel Hughes, Charles Carroll of Carrollton, John Cadwalader, Samuel Chase, John Debutts, George Digges, Philip Key, Gustavus Scot, and Joseph Dashiell, Esquires, to confer with the Virginia deputation on the subject in question.

A meeting of the delegations was held at Annapolis on the 22d, and organized by calling General Washington to the chair, and appointing Randolph B. Latimer, clerk.

Upon assuming the chair, General Washington briefly stated that the object of the meeting was to confer together upon the subject of opening and improving the navigation of the River Potomac, and concerting a plan for opening a proper road between the waters of the Potomac and the most convenient western waters. That the commissioners on the part of the commonwealth of Virginia were fully authorized and prepared to act on this subject with the committee appointed by the General Assembly of Maryland.

The conference then proceeded to take the subject matter referred to them into their consideration; and after a full discussion, and the free interchange of views, a committee was appointed, and after due deliberation submitted the following report, which was unanimously adopted:—

"That it is the opinion of this conference, that the removing the obstructions in the River Potomac, and the making the same capable of navigation from tide-water as far up the north branch of the said river as may be convenient and practicable, will increase the commerce of the commonwealth of Virginia and State of Maryland, and greatly promote the political interests of the United States, by forming a free and easy communication and connection with the people settled on the western waters, already very considerable in their numbers, and rapidly increasing, from the mildness of the climate and the fertility of the soil.

"That it is the opinion of the conference, that the proposal to establish a company for opening the River Potomac, merits the approbation of, and deserves to be patronized by, Virginia and Maryland; and that a similar law ought to be passed by the legislatures of the two governments to promote and encourage so laudable an undertaking.

"That it is the opinion of this conference, that it would be proper for Virginia and Maryland each to become subscribers to the amount of fifty shares, and that such subscription would evince to the public the opinion of the legislatures of the practicability and great utility of the plan, and that the example would encourage individuals to embark in the measure, give vigor and security to so important an undertaking, and be a substantial proof to our brethren of the western territory of our disposition to connect ourselves with them by the strongest bonds of friendship and mutual interest.

"That it is the opinion of this conference, that an act of Assembly of Virginia, 'For opening and extending the navigation of the River Potomac, from Fort Cumberland to tide-water,' ought to be repealed.

"That it is the opinion of this conference, from the best information they have obtained, that a road, to begin about the mouth of Stony River, may be carried in about twenty or twenty-two miles to the Dunker Bottom or Cheat River; from whence, this conference are of opinion, that batteaux navigation may be made, though, perhaps, at considerable expense. That if such navigation cannot be effected by continuing the road about twenty miles further, it would intersect the Monongahela where the navigation is good, and has long been practised.

"That a road from Fort Cumberland to Turkeyfoot would be about thirty-three miles, from whence an improvement of the Youghiogheny River would be necessary, though probably it might be done at less expense than the navigation of the Cheat River could be rendered convenient from the Dunker Bottom.

"That it is a general opinion, that the navigation in the Potomac may be extended to the most convenient point below, or even above the mouth of Stony River, from whence to set off a road to Cheat River; and this conference is satisfied that that road, from the nature of the country through which it may pass, wholly through Virginia and Maryland, will be much better than a road can be made at any reasonable expense from Fort Cumberland to the Youghiogheny, which must be carried through Pennsylvania.

"That it is the opinion of this conference, that if the navigation on the Potomac should be carried to about the mouth of the Stony River, a communication with the western waters, through a road from thence extended even to the Monongahela, would be preferable in most points of view to that by a road from Fort Cumberland to Turkeyfoot, the only other way practicable, and in any degree useful; that the communication by a road from Fort Cumberland to the present navigable parts of the Youghiogheny, and thence through that river, though in the opinion of this conference a second object only, would facilitate the intercourse with a very respectable number of the western settlers, contribute much to their convenience and accommodation, and that the benefits resulting therefrom to these States would compensate the expense of improving that road."

The conferees therefore recommended that the Legislatures of Virginia and Maryland appoint skilful persons to view and accurately examine and survey the Potomac, from Fort Cumberland to the mouth of Stony River, and the River Cheat from about the Dunker Bottom to the present navigable part thereof, and if they judge the navigation can be extended to a convenient distance above Fort Cumberland, that they may from thence survey, lay off, and mark, a road to the Cheat River, or continue the same to the navigation as they may think will most effectually establish the communication between the said eastern and western waters. And that the said road be cut and cleared not less than eighty feet, and properly improved and maintained in repair, not less than forty, nor more than fifty feet wide, at the joint expense of both States; and the conferees begged leave to recommend that each State appropriate three thousand three hundred and thirty-three and one-third dollars for the purpose; and the conference was further of opinion, that the States of Virginia and Maryland request permission of the State of Pennsylvania to lay out and improve a road through such part of that State as might be necessary in the best and most proper direction from Fort Cumberland to the navigable part of the Youghiogheny, and on such permission being obtained, that proper persons be appointed to survey, mark, clear, and improve, such road at the equal expense of Virginia and Maryland.

This interesting report, drawn up under the personal advisement and in conformity with the views of the illustrious chairman, and signed by R. B. Latimer, Clerk, was in due time submitted to the Legislatures of Virginia and Maryland; and forms the basis of the legislative action upon which the POTOMAC COMPANY was incorporated and organized.

The preamble to the act of incorporation declares that the extension of the navigation of the Potomac River from tide-water to the highest place practicable on the north branch will be of great public utility, and many persons are willing to subscribe large sums of money to effect so laudable and beneficial a work, and it is just and proper that they, their heirs and assigns, should be empowered to receive reasonable tolls forever, in satisfaction for the money advanced by them in carrying the work into execution, and the risk they run, and as it may be necessary to cut canals and erect locks and other works on both sides of the river, and the Legislatures of Maryland and Virginia, being impressed with the importance of the object, are desirous of encouraging so useful an undertaking: Therefore enact—

That it shall and may be lawful to open books in the city of Richmond, towns of Alexandria and Winchester, in Virginia, for receiving and entering subscriptions for the said undertaking, under the management of Jaqueline Ambler and John Beckley, at the city of Richmond, of John Fitzgerald and William Hartshorne at the town of Alexandria, and of Joseph Holmes and Edward Smith of the town of Winchester; and in Maryland, in the city of Annapolis, Georgetown, and Fredericktown, under the management of Christopher Richmond and John Davidson, Merchant, or either of them, at the city of Annapolis; William Deakins and Benjamin Stoddert, or either of them, at Georgetown; Joseph Sim and Abraham Faw, or either of them, at Fredericktown; which subscriptions shall be made personally or by power of attorney, and shall be made in Spanish milled dollars, but may be paid in foreign silver or gold coin of the value; that the said books shall be opened for receiving subscriptions on the eighth day of February next, and continue open for this purpose until the tenth day of May next inclusive, and on the seventeenth day of said month of May there shall be a general meeting of the stockholders at the town of Alexandria, of which meeting notice shall be given by the said managers or any four of them in the Virginia and Maryland Gazettes, at least one month next before the said meeting, and such meeting shall and may be continued from day to day until the business is finished, and the acting managers at the time and place hereinafter mentioned shall lay before such of the subscribers as shall meet according to the said notice, the books by them respectively kept, containing the state of the said subscriptions; and if one-half the capital sum hereinafter mentioned should, upon examination, appear not to have been subscribed, then the said managers, at the said meeting, are empowered to take and receive subscriptions to make up the deficiency, and a just and true list of all the subscribers, with the sum subscribed by each, shall be made out and returned by the said managers, or any four or more of them, under their hands, into the General Court of each State, to be there recorded; and in case more than two hundred and twenty two thousand and twenty two dollars and two-ninths of a dollar shall be subscribed, then the same shall be reduced to that sum by the said managers, or a majority of them, by beginning at, and striking off a share from all subscriptions, under the largest and above one share, until the sum is reduced to the capital of two hundred and twenty two thousand and twenty two dollars and two-ninths of a dollar, or until a share is taken from all subscriptions above one share, and lots shall be drawn between the subscribers of equal sums to determine the numbers in which such subscribers shall stand, on a list to be made for striking off as aforesaid; and if the sum subscribed still exceeds the capital aforesaid, then to strike off by the same rule until the sum subscribed is reduced to the capital aforesaid, or all the subscriptions are reduced to one share; and if there still be an excess, then lots to be drawn to determine the subscribers who are to be excluded, to reduce the subscriptions to the capital aforesaid, which striking off shall be certified in the list aforesaid, and the said capital sum shall be reckoned and divided into five hundred shares of four hundred and forty four dollars and four-ninths of a dollar each, of which every person subscribing may take and subscribe for one or more whole shares, and not otherwise: *Provided*, that unless one-half of the said capital shall be subscribed as aforesaid, then the President and Directors are hereby empowered and directed to take and receive the subscriptions which shall first be offered in whole shares as aforesaid, until the deficiency shall be made up, a certificate of which additional subscriptions shall be made under the hands of the President and Directors, or a majority of them for the time being, and returned to and recorded in the General Courts aforesaid.

That in case one-half of the said capital, or a greater sum, shall be subscribed as aforesaid, the said subscribers, and their heirs and assigns, from the time of the said first meeting, shall be and are hereby declared to be incorporated into a company, by the name of the "Potomac Company," and may sue and be sued as such; and such of the said subscribers as shall be present at the said meeting, or a majority of them, are hereby empowered and required to elect a President and four Directors, for conducting the said undertaking, and managing all the said company's business and concerns, for and during such time, not exceeding three years, as the said subscribers, or a majority of them, shall think fit. And in counting the votes of all general meetings of the said company, each member shall be allowed one vote for every share as far as ten shares, and one vote for every five shares above ten, by him or her held at the time in the said company; and any proprietor, by writing under his or her hand, executed before two witnesses, may depute any other member or proprietor to vote and act as proxy for him or her, at any general meeting.

That the said President and Director so elected, and their successors, or a majority of them assembled, shall have full power and authority to agree with any person or persons on behalf of said company, to cut such canals and erect such locks, and perform such other works as they shall judge necessary for opening, improving, and extending the navigation of the said river above tide-water, to the highest part of the North Branch to which navigation can be extended, and carrying on the same, from place to place, and from time to time, and upon such terms and in such manner as they shall think fit; and out of the money arising from the subscriptions and the tolls, and other aids hereinafter given, to pay for the same, and to repair and keep in order the said locks and other works necessary therein, and to defray all incidental charges; and also to appoint a treasurer, clerk, and such other officers, toll-gatherers, managers, and servants as they shall judge requisite, and to agree for and settle their respective wages or allowances, and settle, pass, and sign their accounts, and also to make and establish rules of proceeding, and to transact all the other business and concerns of the said company, in and during the intervals between the general meetings of the same; and they shall be allowed as a satisfaction for their trouble therein, such sum of money as shall, by a general meeting of the subscribers, be determined: *Provided, always*, that the Treasurer shall give bond in such penalty and with such security as the said President and Directors, or a majority of them, shall direct, for the true and faithful discharge of the trust reposed in him, and that the allowance to be made to him for his services shall not exceed three pounds in the hundred, for the disbursements by him made; and that no officer in the said company shall have any vote in the settlement or passing of his own account.

That the said President and Directors and their successors, or a majority of them, shall have full power and authority, from time to time, as money shall be wanted, to make and sign orders for that purpose, and direct at what time, and in what proportion, the proprietors shall advance and pay off the sums subscribed, which orders shall be advertised at least one month in the Virginia and Maryland Gazettes; and they are hereby authorized and empowered to demand and receive of the several proprietors, from time to time, the sums of money so ordered to be advanced for carrying on and executing, or repairing and keeping in order the said works, until the sums to be deposited into the hands of the Treasurer, to be by him disbursed and paid out as the said President and Directors, or a majority of them, shall order and direct. And if any of the said proprietors shall refuse or neglect to pay their said proportions within one month after the same so ordered and advertised as aforesaid, the said President and Directors, or a majority of them, may sell at auction and convey to the purchaser, the share or shares of such proprietor so refusing or neglecting payment, giving at least one month's notice of the sale in the Virginia and Maryland Gazettes, and after retaining the sum due, and charges of sale out of the money produced thereby, they shall refund and pay the overplus, if any, to the former owner; and if such sale shall not produce the full sum ordered and directed to be advanced as aforesaid, with the incidental charges, the said President and Directors, or a majority of them, may in the name of the company, sue for and recover the balance by action of debt, or on the case; and the said purchaser or purchasers shall be subject to the same rules and regulations, as if the said sale and conveyance had been made by the original proprietor, and to continue the succession of the said President and Directors, and to keep up the same number.

That, from time to time, upon the expiration of the said term for which the said President and Directors were appointed, the proprietors of the said company, at the next general meeting, shall either continue the said President and Directors, or any of them, or shall choose others in their stead; and in case of the death, removal, resignation, or incapacity of the President, or any of the said Directors, may and shall, in manner aforesaid, elect any other person or persons, to be President and Directors, in the room of him or them so dying, removing, or resigning; and may at any of their general meetings, remove the President, or any of the Directors, and appoint others, for and during the remainder of the term for which such person or persons were at first to have acted.

That every President and Director, before he acts as such, shall take an oath or affirmation, for the due execution of his office.

That the presence of proprietors, having one hundred shares at the least, shall be necessary to constitute a general meeting; and that there be a general meeting of proprietors on the first Monday in August in every year, at such convenient town as shall, from time to time, be appointed by the said general meeting; but if a sufficient number shall not attend on that day, the proprietors who do attend, may adjourn such meeting from day to day, till a general meeting of proprietors shall be had, which may be continued from day to day, until the business of the company is finished; to which meeting the President and Directors shall make report, and render distinct and just accounts of all their proceedings, and on finding them fairly and justly stated, the proprietors then present, or a majority of them, shall give a certificate thereof, a duplicate of which shall be entered on the said company's books; and at such yearly general meetings, after leaving in the hands of the Treasurer such sum as the proprietors, or a majority of them, shall judge necessary for repairs and contingent charges, an equal dividend of all the net profits, arising from the tolls hereby granted, shall be ordered, and made to and among all the proprietors of the said company, in proportion to their several shares; and upon any emergency in the interval between the said yearly meetings, the said President, or a majority of the said Directors, may appoint a general meeting of the proprietors of the said company, at any convenient town, giving at least one month's previous notice in the Maryland and Virginia Gazettes, which meeting may be adjourned and continued as aforesaid.

That for and in consideration of the expenses the said proprietors will be at, not only in cutting the said canals, erecting locks and other works, for opening the different falls of the said river, and in improving and extending the navigation thereof, but in maintaining and keeping the same in repair, the said canal and works, with all their profits, shall be, and the same are hereby vested in the said proprietors, their heirs and assigns, forever, as tenants in common, in proportion to their respective shares; and the same shall be deemed real estate, and be forever exempt from payment of any tax, imposition, or assessment whatsoever; and it shall and may be lawful for the said President and Directors at all times, forever hereafter, to demand and receive, at the nearest convenient place below the mouth of the South Branch, and at or near Payne's Falls, and at or above the Great Falls of the River Potomac, and every of these places separately, for all commodities, transported through either of them respectively, tolls, according to the following table and rates, to wit:—

COMMODITIES.	TOLLS.								
	At the mouth of the South Branch.			At Payne's Falls.			At the Great Falls.		
	£	s.	d.	£	s.	d.	£	s.	d.
Every pipe or hogshead of wine containing more than 65 gallons	0	1	6	0	1	6	0	3	0
Every hogshead of rum or other spirits	0	1	3	0	1	3	0	2	6
Every hogshead of tobacco	0	1	0	0	1	0	0	2	0
Every cask between 65 and 35 gallons, one-half of a pipe or hogshead; barrels one-fourth part; and smaller casks or kegs in proportion, according to the quality and quantity of their contents of wine or spirits.									
For casks of linseed oil, the same as spirits.									
Every bushel of wheat, peas, beans, or flaxseed	0	0	½	0	0	¼	0	0	1
Every bushel of Indian corn, or other grain or salt	0	0	¼	0	0	¼	0	0	½
Every barrel of pork	0	0	6	0	0	6	0	1	0
Every barrel of beef	0	0	4	0	0	4	0	0	8
Every barrel of flour	0	0	3	0	0	3	0	0	6
Every ton of hemp, flax, potash, bar or manufactured iron	0	2	6	0	2	6	0	5	0
Every ton of pig iron or castings	0	0	10	0	0	10	0	1	8
Every ton of copper, lead, or other ore other than iron ore	0	2	0	0	2	0	0	4	0
Every ton of stone or iron ore	0	0	5	0	0	5	0	0	10
Every hundred bushels of lime	0	1	3	0	1	3	0	2	6
Every chaldron of coals	0	0	5	0	0	5	0	0	10
Every hundred pipe staves	0	0	2¼	0	0	2¼	0	0	4½
Every hundred hogshead staves, or pipe or hogshead heading	0	0	1½	0	0	1½	0	0	3
Every hundred cubic feet of plank or scantling; Every hundred cubic feet of other timber; Every gross hundred weight of all other commodities and packages; And every empty boat or vessel which has not commodities on board to yield so much, except an empty boat or vessel returning, whose load has already paid, at the respective places, the sums fixed at each, in which case she is to repass toll free	0	2	6	0	2	6	0	5	0

which tolls are rated in sterling money, and may be discharged in foreign gold or silver coin of the present fineness at the following rates, to wit :—

	£.	s.	d.
Spanish milled piece of eight, or dollar	0	4	6
Other coined silver, of equal fineness, per ounce	0	5	1¾
English milled crowns	0	5	0
French silver crowns	0	5	0
Johannes, weighing eighteen pennyweights	3	12	0
Half Johannes, weighing nine pennyweights	1	16	0
Moidores, weighing six pennyweights eighteen grains	1	7	0
English Guineas, weighing five pennyweights six grains	1	1	0
French Guineas, weighing five pennyweights five grains	1	0	10
Doubloons, weighing seventeen pennyweights	3	6	3
Spanish pistoles, weighing four pennyweights six grains	0	16	6
French milled pistoles, weighing four pennyweights and four grains	0	16	4
Arabian chequins, weighing two pennyweights three grains	0	8	6
Other gold coin (German excepted) by the pennyweight	0	4	0

It is however provided, that should any of the coins above enumerated, hereafter be rendered less valuable than they are at present, either by lessening their weight, or therewith adding a greater quantity of alloy than is in them respectively at present, then so much of any of the said coins, the value of which is so reduced, to be received for the tolls aforesaid as is equal in value to the said coins in their present state of fineness and weight, shall be payable for the said tolls at their reduced value only. And in case of refusal or neglect to pay the tolls at the time of offering to pass through any of the said places, and previous to the vessel's passing through the same, the collectors of the said tolls may lawfully refuse passage to such vessels; and if any vessel shall pass without paying the said toll, then the said collectors may seize such vessel, wherever found, and sell the same at auction for ready money, which, so far as is necessary, shall be applied towards paying the said toll, and all expenses of seizure and sale, and the balance, if any, shall be paid to the owner, and the person having the direction of such vessel shall be liable for such toll, if the same is not paid by sale of such vessel as aforesaid: *Provided*, that the said proprietors, or a majority of them, holding, at least, three hundred shares, shall have full power and authority, at any general meeting, to lessen the said tolls or any of them; or to determine that any article may pass free of toll.

That the said river, and the works to be erected thereon in virtue of this act, when completed, shall forever thereafter be esteemed and taken to be navigable as a public highway, free for the transportation of all goods, commodities, or produce, whatsoever, on payment of the tolls imposed by this act; and no other toll or tax whatever, for the use of the water of the said river, and the works thereon erected, shall at any time hereafter be imposed, by both or either of the said States, subject, nevertheless, to such regulations as the legislatures of the said States may concur in, to prevent the importation of prohibited goods, or to prevent fraud in evading the payment of duties imposed in both or either of the said States, on goods imported into either of them. And whereas it is necessary for the making of said canal, locks, or other works, that a provision should be made for condemning a quantity of land for the purpose:

That it shall and may be lawful for the said President and Directors, or a majority of them, to agree with the owners of any land through which the said canal is intended to pass, for the purchase thereof, and in case of disagreement, or in case the owner thereof shall be a *feme covert*, under age, non compos, or out of the State, on application to any two justices of the county, in which such land shall lie, the said justices shall issue their warrant under their hands, to the sheriff of their county, to summon a jury of twenty-four inhabitants of his county, of property and reputation, not related to the parties, nor in any manner interested, to meet on the land to be valued, at a day to be expressed in the warrant not less than ten nor more than twenty days thereafter; and the sheriff, upon receiving the said warrant, shall forthwith summon the said jury, and when met, provided that not less than twelve do appear, shall administer an oath or affirmation to every juryman that shall appear "that he will faithfully, justly, and impartially value the land (not exceeding in any case the width of one hundred and forty feet), and all damages the owner thereof shall sustain by the cutting the canal through such land, according to the best of his skill and judgment; and that, in such valuation, he will not spare any person through favor or affection, nor any person grieve through malice, hatred, or ill-will." And the inquisition thereof taken, shall be signed by the sheriff, and some twelve or more of the jury, and returned by the sheriff, to the clerk of his county, to be by him recorded. And upon every such valuation, the jury is hereby directed to describe and ascertain the bounds of the land by them valued, and their valuation shall be conclusive on all persons, and shall be paid by the said President and Directors, to the owner of the land or his legal representative; and on payment thereof, the said company shall be seized in fee of such land, as if conveyed by the owner to them, and their successors by legal conveyance: *Provided, nevertheless*, that if any further damage shall arise to any proprietor of land in consequence of opening such canal, or in erecting such works, than had been before considered and valued, it shall and may be lawful for such proprietor, as often as any such new damage shall happen, by application to, and a warrant from, any two justices of the county where the lands lie, to have such further damage valued by a jury in like manner, and to receive and recover the same of the said President and Directors. But nothing herein shall be taken or construed to entitle the proprietor of any such land to recover compensation for any damages which may happen to any mills, forges, or other water-works or improvements, which shall be begun or erected by such proprietor, after such first valuation, unless the said damage is wilfully or maliciously done by the said President and Directors, or some person by their authority.

That the said President and Directors, or a majority of them, are hereby authorized to agree with the proprietors for the purchase of a quantity of land, not exceeding one acre, at or near each of the said places of receipt of tolls aforesaid, for the purpose of erecting necessary buildings; and in case of disagreement, or any of the disabilities aforesaid, or the proprietor being out of the State, then such land may be valued, condemned, and paid for, as aforesaid, for the purpose aforesaid; and the said company shall, upon payment of the valuation of the said land, be seized thereof in fee simple as aforesaid. And whereas, some of the places through which it may be necessary to conduct the said canals may be convenient for erecting mills, forges, and other water-works, and the persons possessors of such situations may design to improve the same, and it is the intention of this act not to interfere with private property, but for the purpose of improving and perfecting the said navigation.

That the water or any part thereof conveyed through any canal or cut made by the said company, shall not be used for any purpose but navigation, unless the consent of the proprietors of the land through which the same shall be led, be first had; and the said President and Directors, or a majority of them, are hereby empowered and directed, if it can be conveniently done to answer both the purposes of navigation and water-works aforesaid, to enter into reasonable agreements with the proprietors of such situation, concerning the just proportion of the expenses of making large canals or cuts capable of carrying such quantities of water as may be sufficient for the purposes of navigation, and also for any such water-works as aforesaid.

That it shall and may be lawful for every of the said proprietors to transfer his share or shares, by deed, executed before two witnesses, and registered, after proof of the execution thereof, in the said company's books, and not otherwise, except by devise, which devise shall also be exhibited to the President and Directors and registered in the company's books before the devise or devises shall be entitled to draw any part of the profits from the said tolls: *Provided*, that no transfer whatsoever shall be made, except for one or more whole share or shares, and not for part of such shares, and that no share shall at any time be sold, conveyed, transferred, or held, in trust, for the use and benefit, or in the name of another, whereby the said President and Directors or proprietors of the said company, or any of them, shall or may be challenged, or made to answer, concerning any such trust, but that every such person appearing as aforesaid to be proprietor shall, as to the others of the said company, be to every intent taken absolutely as such, but as between any trustee and the person for whose benefit any trust shall be created, the common remedy may be pursued. And whereas it hath been represented to the General Assembly that sundry persons are willing and desirous, on account of the great public advantages and improvement their estates may receive thereby, to promote and contribute towards so useful an undertaking and to subscribe sums of money to be paid on condition the said works are really completed and carried into execution, but do not care to run any risk, or desire to have any property therein:

That the said President and Directors shall be, and are hereby empowered to receive and take in subscriptions, upon the said condition and upon the said works being completed and carried into execution according to the true intent and meaning of this act; that it shall and may be lawful for the said President and Directors, or a majority of them, in case of refusal or neglect of payment, in the name of the company as aforesaid to sue for and recover of the said subscribers, their heirs, executors or administrators, the sums by them respectively subscribed, by action of debt, or upon the case, in any court of record within the State.

That if the said capital, and other aids already granted by this act, shall prove insufficient, it shall and may be lawful for the said company, from time to time, to increase the said capital by the addition of as many more whole shares as shall be judged necessary by the said proprietors, or a majority of them, holding at least three hundred shares, present at any general meeting of the said company. And the said President and Directors, or a majority of them, are hereby empowered and required, after giving at least one month's notice thereof in the Maryland and Virginia Gazettes, to open books at the before-mentioned places for receiving and entering such additional subscriptions, in which the proprietors of the said company for the time being, shall and are hereby declared to have the preference of all others for the first thirty days, after the said books shall be opened as aforesaid, of taking and subscribing for so many whole shares as any of them shall choose. And the said President and Directors are hereby required to observe in all other respects the same rules therein, as are by this act prescribed, for receiving and adjusting first the subscriptions, and in like manner to return, under the hands of any three or more of them, an exact list of such additional subscribers, with the sums by them respectively subscribed, into the general courts aforesaid, to be there recorded, and all proprietors of such additional sums shall, and are hereby declared to be, from thenceforward, incorporated into the said company.

That the tolls hereinbefore allowed, to be demanded and received at the nearest convenient place below the mouth of the South Branch are granted, and shall be paid on condition only, that the Potomac Company shall make the river well capable of being navigated in dry seasons, by vessels drawing one foot water, from the place on the North Branch at which a road shall set off to the Cheat River, agreeably to the determination of the Assemblies of Virginia and Maryland, to and through the place which may be fixed on, below the mouth of the South Branch, for receipt of the tolls aforesaid; but if the said river is only navigable as aforesaid from Fort Cumberland, to and through the said place below the mouth of the South Branch, then only two-thirds of the said tolls shall be there received. That the tolls hereinbefore allowed, to be demanded and received at or near Payne's Falls are granted and shall be payable on condition only, that the said Potomac Company shall make the river well capable of being navigated in dry seasons, by vessels drawing one foot water, from the place of collection, near the mouth of the South Branch to and through Payne's Falls as aforesaid. That the tolls hereinbefore allowed to be demanded and received at the Great Falls, are granted, and shall be payable on condition only that the said Potomac Company shall make the river well capable of being navigated in dry seasons, from Payne's Falls to the Great Falls, by vessels drawing one foot water, and from the Great Falls to tide-water, and shall, at or near the Great Falls, make a cut or canal, twenty-five feet wide, and four feet deep, with sufficient locks, if necessary, each of eighty feet in length, sixteen feet in breadth, and capable of conveying vessels or rafts drawing four feet water at the least, and shall make, at or near the Little Falls, such canal and locks, if necessary, as will be sufficient and proper to let vessels and rafts aforesaid into tide-water, or render the said river navigable in the natural course.

And it is hereby provided, that in case the said company shall not begin the said work within one year after the company shall be formed, or if the navigation shall not be made and improved between the Great Falls and Fort Cumberland, in the manner hereinbefore mentioned within three years after the said company shall be formed, that then the said company shall not be entitled to any benefit, privilege or advantage under this act. And in case the said company shall not complete the navigation through and from the Great Falls, to tide-water as aforesaid, within ten years after the said company shall be formed, then shall all interest of the said company and all preference in their favor, as to the navigation and tolls, at, through, and from, the Great Falls to tide-water, be forfeited, and cease.

That all commodities of the produce of either of the said States, or of the western country, which may be carried or transported through the said locks, canals, and river, may be landed, sold, or otherwise disposed of, free from any other duties, impositions, regulations, or restrictions of any kind, than the like commodities of the produce of the State in which the same may happen to be so landed, sold, shipped, or disposed of.

That the Treasurer of this commonwealth shall be authorized and directed to subscribe to the amount of fifty shares in behalf of the same, and the money necessary in consequence of such subscription, shall be paid as the same shall be required. And the Treasurer for the time being shall have a right to vote according to such shares, in person or by proxy, appointed by him, and shall receive the proportion of the tolls aforesaid, which shall from time to time become due to this State for the shares aforesaid.

That so much of every act and acts within the purview of this act, shall be, and the same is, hereby repealed.

An Act for vesting in George Washington, Esq., a certain interest in the companies established for opening and extending the Navigation of the Potomac and James Rivers.

Passed October, 1784.

Whereas, it is the desire of the representatives of this commonwealth (Va.) to embrace every suitable occasion of testifying their sense of the unexampled merits of George Washington, Esq., towards his country, and it is their wish, in particular, that those great works for its improvement, which, both as springing from the liberty which he has been so instrumental in establishing, and as encouraged by his patronage, will be durable monuments of his glory, may be made monuments also of the gratitude of his country.

Be it enacted by the General Assembly, that the Treasurer be directed, in addition to the subscriptions he is hereby authorized to make, to the respective undertakings for opening the navigation of Potomac and James Rivers, to subscribe to the amount of fifty shares to the former, and a hundred shares to the latter, to be paid in like manner with the subscriptions above mentioned; and that the shares so subscribed be, and the same are hereby vested in George Washington, Esquire, his heirs and assigns forever, in as effectual a manner as if the subscriptions had been made by himself or by his attorney.

General Washington's Reply to the Letter of the Governor of Virginia, transmitting a copy of the foregoing Act of the General Assembly.

Dear Sir: Your excellency having been pleased to transmit to me a copy of the act appropriating to my benefit certain shares in the companies for opening the navigation of James and Potomac Rivers, I take the liberty of returning to the General Assembly, through your hands, the profound and grateful acknowledgments inspired by so signal a mark of their beneficent intentions towards me. I beg you, sir, to assure them that I am filled on this occasion with every sentiment which can flow from a heart warm with love for my country; sensible to every token of its approbation and affection, and solicitous to testify, in every instance, a respectful submission to its wishes. With these sentiments in my bosom, I need not dwell on the anxiety I feel in being obliged, in this instance, to decline a favor which is rendered no less flattering by the manner in which it is conveyed, than it is affectionate in itself. In explaining this obligation, I pass over a comparison of my endeavors in the public service with the many honorable testimonies of approbation which have already so far overrated and overpaid them; reciting one consideration only, which supersedes the necessity of recurring to every other. When I was first called to the station with which I was honored during the late conflict for our liberties, to the diffidence which I had so many reasons to feel in accepting it, I thought it my duty to join a former resolution to shut my hand against every pecuniary recompense ; to this resolution I have invariably adhered ; from this resolution (if I had the inclination) I do not consider myself at liberty to depart. Whilst I repeat, therefore, my fervent acknowledgments to the legislature for their very kind sentiments and intentions in my favor, and at the same time beg them to be persuaded, that a remembrance of this singular proof of their goodness towards me, will never cease to cherish returns of the warmest affection and gratitude, I must pray that their act, so far as it has for its object my personal emolument, may not have its effect. But if it should please the General Assembly to permit me to turn the destination of the fund vested in me, from my private emolument to objects of a public nature, it will be my study, in selecting these, to prove the sincerity of my gratitude for the honor conferred on me, by preferring such as may appear most subservient to the enlightened and patriotic views of the legislature.

In accordance with the wishes so patriotically presented by the reply of General Washington to the Governor of Virginia, the act was repealed during the same session; and it was further enacted that the said shares, with the tolls and profits hereafter accruing therefrom, should stand appropriated to such objects of a public nature, in such manner, and under such distributions as General Washington, by deed during his life, or by his last will and testament, should direct and appoint.

A short time after the expiration of the period which was specified for receiving subscriptions to the capital stock, a general meeting was called to ascertain the number of shares that were taken, and if sufficient, formally to organize the company by the election of officers.

A sufficient number of shares having been subscribed, a meeting was held in pursuance to previous public notice published in some of the Maryland and Virginia Gazettes, at Alexandria, on the 17th day of May, 1785.

An unusual degree of public feeling was already manifested in the proposed management of the affairs of the company. It was an enterprise of a novel character, and prompted more by the impulse of patriotic considerations, than by the influence of anticipated pecuniary advantages to the subscribers; it had enlisted in its success some of the most prominent and distinguished men of the two sister States. The meeting was regarded with no ordinary concern. Public spirited individuals from several parts of Virginia and Maryland proceeded to Alexandria to witness its proceedings. The city presented a spectacle which at that early day was seldom witnessed. The general belief that the immortal Washington, the man who had borne his country in triumph through the storms of the Revolutionary War, and achieved its national independence, would accept the office of President of the company, was of itself calculated to impart an extraordinary interest to the occasion. When the hour for opening the meeting had arrived, a large number of citizens were in attendance. The meeting was called to order by one of the proprietors, and was subsequently organized by electing Daniel Carrol, Esquire, Chairman, and Charles Lee, Esquire, Clerk.

Upon the presentation of the subscription books, it was ascertained that the shares subscribed were—

Virginia.		
In the Richmond Book	100	Shares.
Alexandria, do	135	do
Winchester, do	31	do
Maryland.		
Annapolis, do	73	do
Georgetown, do	42	do
Frederick, do	22	do

amounting to four hundred and three shares, making a capital of forty thousand three hundred pounds sterling money.

On motion, it was then resolved, That the subscribers present in person and by proxy, proceed to the choice of President and Directors, who shall continue in office until the first Monday in the month of August 1786, and that at every general meeting, in taking the votes of the proprietors, each proprietor shall give in his vote or votes at the Clerk's table, in writing, and where the vote or votes shall be given by proxy, that the name of each constituent shall also be inserted.

The chairman then suggested to the meeting the importance of an examination of the deputations and the proxies before the election, and appointed Charles Sims and James Keith as the examining committee. This committee having discharged the duties of their appointment, reported that the deputations from Thomas Blackburn to William Brown, from Thomas Johnson to Abraham Farr, and from John Lyon to Abraham Farr, were illegal and insufficient, and executed only before one witness, and could not be admitted to vote at this election. The report was adopted.

The proprietors present in person and those who were absent, but legally represented by proxies, then proceeded to the choice of President and four Directors, and on examining and counting the votes, a majority was in favor of his Excellency George Washington to be President, and Thomas Johnston, Thomas Sim Lee, John Fitzgerald and George Gilpin, Esquires, to be Directors, and thereupon the chairman declared his excellency George Washington President, and Thomas Johnston, Thomas Sim Lee, John Fitzgerald and George Gilpin, Esquires, Directors of the Potomac Company.

This announcement of the result of the election was received by the meeting with unbounded joy and satisfaction.

The papers, forms, and proxies in the hands of the several deputations, and the subscription books, as also the minutes of the meeting, were then placed in charge of the President and Directors, and, after designating the day and place for the first meeting of the Board, the meeting adjourned.

The Board, agreeably to appointment, met in Alexandria on Monday the 30th day of May, 1785, to be duly qualified.

Present: Gen. GEORGE WASHINGTON, *President.*

GEORGE GILPIN, JOHN FITZGERALD, THOMAS SIM LEE, and THOMAS JOHNSTON, *Directors.*

George Gilpin administered the oath of office prescribed by the General Assemblies of Virginia and Maryland to George Washington, John Fitzgerald, Thomas Sim Lee, and Thomas Johnston; and John Fitzgerald administered the oath of office to George Gilpin.

The Board having been qualified, proceeded to the selection of individuals for treasurer and clerk, and appointed William Hartshorne, of Alexandria, treasurer, and John Potts, Jun., of the same place, clerk. The former allowed three per cent. upon the disbursements as a compensation for his services, and to enter into a bond in the penalty of ten thousand pounds sterling, with two good and sufficient securities, to be approved by the Board. The latter to be paid twenty one shillings sterling for each day he shall attend the Board, besides his reasonable expenses when he occasionally attends the sittings or sessions of the Board out of Alexandria, and thereby incurs an extraordinary expense.

The company, now fully organized, entered upon

the commencement of its active duties with flattering prospects of success. With the illustrious Washington at its head, and the encouragement of the most distinguished men of Maryland and Virginia among its subscribers, the enterprise was one of extreme interest both to the company and the public.

When the members of the Board were assembled—the President offered his congratulations upon the happy condition which brought them together, and in brief and eloquent terms animated their zeal, in the prosecution of the enterprise by his own unbounded patriotism and public spirit.

Many suggestions were submitted and discussed relative to the most eligible plan for practical operations; and it was at length agreed: to divide the line of the river to be improved into two sections; the first or *lower* section to extend from tide water to the upper part of the Shenandoah Falls—and the upper section include the river between the upper part of the Shenandoah Falls, and the highest point practicable upon the North Branch, and to which the improvement could be extended and made navigable.

To each of these sections was assigned a general director, skilled in the character of the work to be performed, one suitable assistant, three overseers, and fifty men.

To obtain the services of the most competent and skilful men to conduct the opening and improving the navigation, the Board directed advertisements to be inserted in the Alexandria, Baltimore, and one or more of the Philadelphia papers, giving notice that it would meet at Alexandria on the first day of July next "to agree with two persons who best understood the character of the work to be done, and its management, to the greatest advantage."

On account of the toilsome character of the work, the ordinary wages of that day were not sufficient inducements to the laboring classes to enter into the service of the company. A more liberal scale of allowance was accordingly adopted; and in addition to the advance upon the wages, good and substantial provisions were supplied and a reasonable quantity of spirits. As a further encouragement to the hands, it was proposed to add yet more to the wages of those who were most dexterous and skilful in boring and blowing rocks, and the conductor was directed to be at Seneca on the 1st and at Shenandoah on the 14th of July, to examine such as would offer for this service.

In the mean time, the Clerk was directed to write a letter to Capt. Abraham Sheppard, of Sheppardstown, requesting him to contract for the building of two *very* strong boats for the use of the company, each to be thirty five feet long, eight feet wide or upwards, and not less than twenty inches deep, in the common manner of the flats used at the ferries on the Potomac above tide-water.

A similar letter was written to Col. James Clapham, in whose judgment and experience in the construction of boats, the President and Directors entertained the greatest confidence.

The character of the river above Payne's Falls was at this time little known. From the junction of the Shenandoah to the sources of the North Branch was an almost uninterrupted wilderness, and few persons had penetrated the gorges and passes of the numerous mountain ranges through which it had forced its way. But one individual connected with the enterprise of the Potomac Company, had perhaps ever viewed the bold and picturesque scenery which bordered upon the stream, or the rocks and falls that broke its surface. To have a correct view of the difficulties that would be encountered in the progress of the improvement of its navigation, it was important that the members of the Board should possess a *personal* knowledge of the part of the river to be improved, and it was accordingly determined to proceed to an examination, immediately after the general meeting in August next.

The selection of persons to fill the subordinate stations in the company, was a matter of much solicitude. After repeated notifications through the columns of the public press in Philadelphia, Virginia, and Maryland, inviting the attention of suitable individuals to the subject, and the personal efforts of many of the subscribers, superadded to the very liberal allowances that were offered, having all failed of success, Col. Gilpin, a member of the Board, was specially delegated with full power and authority to act on this subject in behalf of the company.

Believing that a personal interview with applicants would be most likely attended with success, he gave public notice that he would be at Seneca and Shenandoah Falls on the 14th of July ensuing, to meet such persons as would offer for the stations that were specified, and if, upon proper examination of their credentials, and a satisfactory conviction of their capacity and integrity, were adjudged worthy of the appointment, he would at once, under the authority vested in him, confer it upon them, and fix the time when the work should commence.

The next annual meeting of the Board was held, agreeably to previous notice, in Georgetown, on the 1st day of August, 1785.

Present: Gen. GEORGE WASHINGTON, *President.*

THOMAS S. LEE, JOHN FITZGERALD, THOMAS JOHNSTON, GEORGE GILPIN, *Directors.*

The first business in order was the examination of sundry accounts amounting to £182 7*s.* 4*d.*, which, having been found correct, the Treasurer was directed to pay.

It was also ordered that the Treasurer forthwith advance to Mr. James Rumsey, the principal manager, the sum of fifty pounds, Virginia currency, as a contingent fund, and to be expended in small sums for the use of the company, and at stated periods to render an account accompanied by the vouchers.

The subject which mainly occupied the attention of the Board at this meeting, was the accountability of the subordinate officers relative to the disbursements of money. The arrangement that had been made for commencing the work, required the adoption of a rigid system, and from which no departure could be admitted under any circumstances upon the mere option of an assistant or overseer—nor by the authority of the principal manager, independent of the subsequent action of the Board. The plan was simple and efficient. Each overseer was directed to keep a book in which the name of every person employed was enrolled, with columns properly ruled for an exact account of the days on which each hand was employed, and also of the days when absent, and every fortnight he was required to render an account to the assistant manager, who, if he approved the same, to certify thereto, and present it to the principal manager, and if he also approved of the account, it should be authority to the Treasurer to furnish such sum of money as would be sufficient to discharge the account.

After the transaction of the most important business of the meeting, and it had adjourned, the President and members of the Board proceeded to the Shenandoah Falls for the purpose of making the examination that would enable them to decide upon the kind of improvement to overcome the difficulties the Falls presented in the navigation of the river. Viewing the *still water* above and below, and the character of the obstructions in the Falls, the members were unanimously of the opinion that no lock would be required, and that nothing more was necessary than the removal of the rocks that were irregularly scattered over the Falls; and a party was organized to clear and improve the navigation from Payne's upwards, through the Shenandoah Falls, and placed under the direction of Mr. Rumsey, the principal director, whom Col. Gilpin had just appointed.

The following letter of instructions was written to him by the President:—

SHENANDOAH FALLS, 3d day of August, 1785.

SIR: As you have attended the President and Directors in their view and examination of the river, from the upper part of the Seneca Falls to the Great Falls, and from the flat water above to the flat water below the Shenandoah Falls, you are possessed not only of their opinion of the course in general to be improved, and their idea of effecting the work, but also of their sentiments on many particular spots. The President and Directors have no doubt, could they personally attend the work in its progress, and see the river at those places in its different situations, they might in many instances depart from their present opinions. The nature of the work and our situations make it therefore necessary to leave it to your discretion to vary from what you may have conceived our opinion to be as to the tract or manner of executing the work, and we do it the more cheerfully, as you seem to be equally impressed as ourselves with the importance of a straight navigation, and the advantages of avoiding, as far as well may be, to cross currents. The opportunity you will have to watch the water at different heights, and your industry in examining more minutely the different obstructions, will enable you to exercise the discretionary power left with you, to your own credit and our satisfaction.

You are already apprised of our change of resolution as to the plan of working the upper party, and the reasons which induced that change, and as effecting the navigation through the Shenandoah and Seneca Falls, will be immediately advantageous to a great extent of country, you are not to consider yourself restricted to the number of fifty hands for each party, but you are to employ as many as you have an opportunity to engage, and you can work to advantage, so that the work may be expedited ; but you must immediately, on exceeding one hundred in the whole, give information to the President, lest any disappointment should happen in the ready payment of the company's debts, which by all means is to be avoided.

For the President and Directors,

G. WASHINGTON, *P.*

Upon the receipt of this letter of instructions from General Washington, Mr. Rumsey immediately prepared himself to carry its purposes into effect, and although much was left to his discretion, he found few occasions to depart from the line marked out for him to pursue. It required a personal knowledge of the river for a succession of years, and at its different stages of water, to form an adequate idea of the best *course* for the contemplated improvement. Of this the Board were fully satisfied, and the discretionary power which was given to Mr. Rumsey on account of his intimate knowledge of the river and its condition from the lowest stages of water to the highest freshets, and his active and energetic character, the members felt every assurance that the responsibility and trust they devolved upon him could not be committed to better hands.

The first object to which his attention was directed, was to *trace* out the line or channel of the river to be cleared and improved, and which he then divided into *parts*, to each of which he assigned a specified number of hands, under the charge of an overseer.

The hands were accordingly distributed upon the line, and were soon at work. The condition of the water was favorable for prosecuting the improvement with energy and zeal, and the organization seemed to be well calculated for active operations.

Notwithstanding the favorable circumstances under which the company was organized, the liberal allowance to the workmen for their services, and the disposition of the Board and of the principal conductor to abate the severity of the labor by granting every reasonable indulgence, one month had scarcely elapsed before a turbulent and insubordinate spirit was manifested among the hands, and to a degree as to require immediate and signal correction. Irregularity, misconduct, and insolent behavior placed the authority of the conductor and his subordinates at defiance. The work that was directed to be done was either entirely omitted or but partially performed, and it was evident to the conductor that not much progress could be made in improving the navigation, unless at least one-half of the laborers then on the line were discharged and the number replaced by others more orderly and obedient. Mr. Rumsey was not long in deciding upon the course to be pursued. He made a report of all the facts relative to the insubordination of the workmen to General Washington in a written communication, and expressed his hope that it would receive the earliest attention. Upon the receipt of this communication, a meeting of the Board was called at Alexandria on the 9th of September, 1785, and after a full exposition of the difficulties among the hands, it was unanimously declared, as the opinion (of the Board) "that it would facilitate the work to purchase sixty servants for the use of the company;" and the Secretary was directed to open a correspondence with some person in Baltimore and in Philadelphia to ascertain the best terms upon which they could be procured.

As soon as the Secretary had received replies to his letters, he advised the President of the company, who thereupon called a meeting of the Board at Alexandria, Sept. 26th, 1785.

Present: Gen. GEORGE WASHINGTON, *President.*

GEO. GILPIN, JOHN FITZGERALD, *Directors.*

Sundry accounts properly authenticated, amounting to £182 8*s.* 3*d.*, were presented and passed, and the Treasurer was directed to pay them.

The subject for which the meeting was particularly called was then introduced by the President, and the report he had received from Mr. Rumsey, and the answers from Philadelphia and Baltimore to the letters from the Secretary were read; and, after due deliberation and discussion, it was finally ordered that the Secretary be directed to write letters to Messrs. Stewart & Plunket, of Baltimore, and Mr. John Maxwell Nesbit, of Philadelphia, the gentlemen to whom the Secretary had previously made application, "to purchase for the use of the company sixty servants, and to request of each of them, that as soon as there may be an arrival at either place, out of which the number can probably be procured, immediately to send an express at the expense of the company, with information of it, that they may avail themselves of the first opportunity of getting them out, and also to prevent a purchase being made at both places."

In the mean time, it was important that the enterprise should be prosecuted with as much energy and assiduity as the circumstances under which the company was then placed would allow. The water in the river was unusually low, and the obstructions to be removed from the channel were discoverable throughout the almost entire length to be improved. It was also a season of extraordinary health in the valley of the Potomac, and provisions were abundant and cheap,

Influenced by these considerations, the Board declared it as their unanimous opinion that Mr. Rumsey, the conductor, should engage such of the hands as deserve encouragement, to continue in the service of the company on the best terms he could obtain from them, and until the further order of the Board; and that a meeting of the Board of President and Directors be held at Georgetown, in the State of Maryland, on Monday the seventeenth day of October next, of which notice to be given to the Directors, and also to Mr. Rumsey and Mr. Stewart, the principal and the assistant managers.

On the 10th of October, notice was accordingly transmitted to the several members to attend a meeting of the Board in Georgetown on the day proposed, to take the existing condition of the affairs of the company into consideration, and to adopt such measures as would more effectually secure the proprietors against the recurrence of the interruptions which had several times seriously checked the progress of the improvement of the channel of the Potomac.

In consequence of the absence of one of the members, the Board was not organized until the 18th of October, when it met at the Great Falls of the Potomac River.

Present: Gen. GEORGE WASHINGTON, *President.*

JOHN FITZGERALD, GEORGE GILPIN, THOS. LEE, and THOS. JOHNSTON, *Directors.*

The President made a detailed statement of the causes which had urged him to call a special meeting, submitting to them such considerations as he deemed appropriate to the occasion, and earnestly invoked the action of the Board on the subject.

The session continued during two days. Many suggestions were made and discussed, opinions were freely expressed, and after a frank and candid consideration of all the facts presented by the principal superintendent, in whom entire confidence was entertained, it was ordered:—

That one hundred good and able working negroes should be hired for the use of the company, for each of whom there should be an allowance of twenty pounds, Virginia currency, also clothing, and to pay their levies and furnish them with rations, viz: 1 lb. salt pork, $1\frac{1}{4}$ lb. salt beef, or $1\frac{1}{2}$ lb. fresh beef or mutton, and a sufficiency of bread each day, and also a reasonable quantity of spirits, when necessary.

That the negroes are to come well clothed, or to be supplied with what may be deficient, which is to be stopped out of the next year's clothing.

It was also ordered:—

That the monthly wages of the men should remain as heretofore, but without making a deduction for the time the weather would not admit of their working.

The applications were requested to be made to Mr. William Hartshorne, in Alexandria, or to Mr. James Rumsey, the principal superintendent, who were duly authorized to enter into contracts for the hands:—

Before the adjournment, the following accounts were presented and directed to be paid.

	£	s.	d.
Josias Clapham	£43	5*s.*	0*d.*
John Potts, Jr.	6	8	3
John Fitzgerald	2	2	0

It was not long before a sufficient number of hands were engaged, and divided into three working parties viz: at the Great Falls, at the Seneca Falls, and at the Shenandoah Falls.

The improvements of the channel at these important points were pushed with due energy and zeal. Some of the largest rocks in the two upper falls were sufficiently blasted, and their fragments generally removed from the channel before a rise in the river compelled a suspension of the work. In the early part of November the river began to rise, and soon overflowed its banks. Much rain had fallen, and the mountain streams at and near the heads of the North and South Branches of the Potomac became unusually high, and one of the most extraordinary freshets in the river was the result.

Driven by the high water the majority of the hands were compelled to abandon their work, and were directed to proceed to the Great Falls, where they were to be occupied in building huts for the accommodation of the men during the winter.

Mr. Rumsey was also authorized to contract for the building of two boats for the use of the company, on such construction as he should think "most advantageous for forwarding the work, and as many more boats on the plan of those formerly constructed as he should deem indispensably necessary."

Many accounts remaining unsettled, the President, before the Board adjourned, requested them to be rendered to the office of the Treasurer, in Alexandria, as soon as they could be prepared. On the 21st November, 1785, accounts with proper vouchers were brought before the Committee of Directors, passed, and ordered to be paid, amounting to £260 15*s.* 5*d.*

The rainy weather was of an unusually long duration, and it was not probable, from the advanced period of the season, that much more work could be done in the channel of the river during the remaining part of the fall. The general superintendent was accordingly instructed to concentrate the working parties at the Great Falls where it was contemplated to engage them in excavating the prism of the canal around the falls, and in the building of ordinary boats.

Much diversity of opinion prevailed as to the most feasible line for the canal. The character of the ground generally was good, but the particular locality of the down lock and its embouchure into the River below the falls required a more particular examination and survey of the route than had yet been given. Personal examinations were made by the several members of the Board, and it was finally directed that an accurate draft of the "track for the proposed canal be made with the courses and distances and also of the "different *risings* and *fallings* in the ground," and that it be prepared in time to be submitted to the Board at the meeting to be held at the Great Falls in March following.

It was also ordered that as soon as the place for taking out the water from the river should be determined on, all the hands not otherwise engaged to be employed in opening that part of the canal, and to continue the excavation to the level of the bed of the river.

Before the adjournment of the meeting, a letter was also read to the Board from William Lyles & Co. proposing to furnish "what rum might be necessary for the use of the hands employed by the company on the river." The offer was liberal, and was accepted for supplying those engaged below the Shenandoah Falls at two shillings per gallon until the further order of the Board.

The surveys directed to be made were immediately commenced—sections and cross sections were run, and very minute and accurate drafts of the ground were prepared, presenting at a glance the elevations and depressions, the *cutting* and *filling* that would be required in the adoption of either of the two routes to which the attention and labor of the *surveying* and *examining* party was directed.

During the interval between this meeting and the time appointed for the next, the attention of the President was much occupied in awakening the public mind to the importance of prosecuting the work which had been so generously undertaken by the proprietors of the company. The original motive which actuated the stockholders seemed for some cause to have abated, and it required the *master spirit* of the enterprise to be exerted, to prevent at this important and critical juncture, a total abandonment of the project. With the powerful influence of the illustrious head of the Potomac Company the cloud which for a brief time hung over its future prospects was dispelled, and new hopes cheered and animated its affairs. The State of Maryland had failed to pay the sums due on the shares it held, and a large number of individual stockholders had also neglected to meet their instalments. The funds of the company were nearly exhausted. The treasury was no longer able to liquidate the claims of individuals against it, and a total prostration of its credit seemed inevitable unless soon relieved. This relief fortunately was afforded under the energetic action of the President and Board of Directors, who had a meeting at the Great Falls on the 1st and 2d days of March, 1786.

Having before them the Report of Mr. William Hartshorne, of Alexandria, the Treasurer of the company, which gave a full and interesting statement of the finances, they devoted two days to the consideration of the best means to obtain funds to continue the improvement of the navigation of the river. To fail of success was an abandonment of the enterprise, and might bring discredit upon the proprietors; every honorable effort was suggested and discussed, and it was finally ordered: "That the Treasurer send an express to Annapolis to make application for payment of the sums due on shares which have been subscribed for by the State, and also to such others as have not been made agreeable to a former order of this Board, and that he send to such persons in the neighborhood of Alexandria as have been delinquents, and also that he write to other defaulters who are at a distance, on the subject."

It was also ordered that the subscribers and proprietors of the company pay into the hands of William Hartshorne, the Treasurer, ten pounds sterling on each respective share on or before the fifteenth day of April next, and the further sum of ten pounds sterling on or before the fifteenth day of June next.

These applications were not disregarded. Many of the proprietors, immediately after receiving the notice, transmitted the sums declared to be due on the 15th of April—with assurances of the payment of the second assessment two months thereafter.

With this encouraging prospect before them, the President and Board entered into arrangements to extend the line of operations. The number of hands was increased, additional working parties were organized, and Mr. James Smith was appointed an assistant manager for one year, to superintend the work upon the same terms and with the same allowance granted to Mr. Richardson Stewart, the first assistant.

Before the President and members of the Board

left the Great Falls, they made a very minute personal examination of the several routes which were marked out by the surveying party to get below the Falls, and they determined to adopt *that* which was traced between the river and Falls Island, as the most eligible. A large party was at once employed in the excavation, and the work was carried on with commendable energy and force.

It was also determined to give public notice that proposals would be received until the meeting of the 15th April to furnish the men employed at and below the Shenandoah with rations for one year. The advertisement was first published in the Alexandria papers on the 3d of March, 1786.

On the 15th day of April, the President called a meeting of the Board at Alexandria, to act upon the several proposals that were received to supply the rations. The terms offered were generally favorable, and the contract was awarded to Mr. Abel Westfall, at the rate of one shilling, Virginia currency, for each ration, who immediately after, with his sureties for the faithful performance of the contract, John Reynolds and Patrick Murray, executed the necessary bond.

The annual meeting of the subscribers was appointed for the 7th day of August, 1786, for the election of a President and Directors for the ensuing year, and to that day the meeting of the Board was adjourned to make their annual report.

ALEXANDRIA, August 7, 1786.

The President and Directors of the Potomac Company beg leave to report that they have called for four dividends on the several subscriptions, as follows:—

The 1st	of	5	per cent.
2d	"	$2\frac{1}{2}$	" "
3d	"	10	" "
4th	"	10	" "

Amounting in the whole to twelve thousand, four hundred and thirty pounds sterling, of which there has been paid five thousand nine hundred and forty pounds sterling.

The several expenditures will appear by the Treasurer's account, who has in hand one thousand six hundred and thirty-six pounds 18*s.* 7*d.* Virginia currency, equal to one thousand two hundred and twenty-seven pounds 10*s.* 2*d.* sterling.

With respect to the business, we beg leave to refer to the Secretary's books, which contain all our orders relating thereto.

In consequence of these orders the work has been carried on at the Seneca and Shenandoah Falls while the waters were low enough to admit of it. After the river rose too high, the hands were removed to the Great Falls, where a considerable progress has been made in cutting a canal, and the most of the men are still employed on account of the uncommon wet season.

We beg leave to remind the subscribers that this is the day appointed by law for electing a President and Directors for the ensuing year.

In behalf of the Directors,

G. WASHINGTON, *P.*

This being the day for the general meeting of the company, a sufficient number of the members appeared to constitute an organization for business. Doctor

David Stewart was appointed Chairman, and Charles Lee, Esq., Secretary.

General Washington presented to the Chairman the report of the President and Directors for the past year, which being read and approved of, was ordered to be entered on the minutes of the company.

The members then proceeded to the annual election of a President and four Directors, when the following named gentlemen were elected:—

General Washington, *President.*

Thomas Johnston, Thomas S. Lee, George Gilpin, John Fitzgerald, *Directors.*

A committee consisting of Col. Robt. T. Hooe, Capt. John Thos. Boucher, and Col. William Syles, were appointed to examine the Treasurer's account, and Directors' books of proceeding for the past year, and also to receive an account from each of the Directors of their expenditures, and to make report thereof to the meeting.

These duties having been performed, they reported, "that they had carefully perused the books of proceedings and orders, from which it appeared to them, that the affairs and business of the company was directed and managed with great attention, care, and ability; and in their opinion the President and Directors ought to be allowed out of the money of the company for their expenses in going to, attending at, and returning from their different meetings as follows, viz:—

GEN. WASHINGTON,	Thirty-four pounds, ten shillings.
THOMAS JOHNSTON, ESQ.,	Thirty pounds.
THOMAS SIM LEE, ESQ.,	Twenty-two pounds, ten shillings.
JOHN FITZGERALD, ESQ.,	Thirty-four pounds, ten shillings.
GEORGE GILPIN, ESQ.,	Thirty-four pounds, ten shillings.

It being in proportion to the time each has attended, at thirty shillings Virginia currency per day."

The report was unanimously adopted, and in testimony of the high sense the company entertained of the faithful and attentive manner the President, Directors and Treasurer discharged their respective trusts, James Keith, Charles Simms, and David Stuart, Esqs., were appointed to return their thanks to those gentlemen.

The time allowed by the charter for completing the navigation from the Great Falls to Fort Cumberland, not being sufficient, and the importance of fixing to it a limit with some degree of certainty, the subscribers were induced to pass a resolution requesting the President and Directors to make an exploration of that part of the river for the purpose of presenting the facts of the difficulties yet to be removed from the channel, to the legislatures of Maryland and Virginia, and to ask for an extension of a definite period to consummate (K) the enterprise.

The stockholders also acted on a petition of Michael Bowman, who superintended the blasting of rocks. He had received a serious injury by the accidental explosion of gunpowder at the Shenandoah Falls while in the service of the company. The justice and liberality of the company is sufficiently exemplified by the fact that relief was granted him, that the President and Directors were not limited in the relief to be afforded by a specific amount, but were authorized and requested to allow him such support from *time* to *time* as to them should seem *reasonable.*

This is the first and only circumstance of the kind which is recorded in the proceedings of the Board, and as it illustrates the humanity and the generosity of the proprietors, is of sufficient interest to be given in the compilation.

A few days after the adjournment, all the arrangements were made for the proposed exploration of the river. The best boats were selected and put in good condition. Provisions, compass, sounding and measuring lines, and such other articles as were necessary to complete equipage were all provided, and on the morning of the 20th day of August, the convoy left the shores upward bound. A more beautiful morning could not have been chosen. Favored with a pleasant breeze and a cloudless sky, the *voyageurs* took their departure with anticipations of pleasure in the performance of an important service, and which were fully realized. The broad surface of the river, the bold and broken banks, the headlands and promontories, the falls and rapids, the wild and picturesque scenery which characterizes the bounding shores of the Potomac, were all calculated earnestly to engage the attention of the party, and materially to abate the severity of the service they had undertaken to perform. A very minute examination of the river was made, and they traced out, as they ascended the stream, and as far as it was practicable, the line of the channel remaining to be improved. After an absence of four days in this arduous and laborious duty, the party returned to the Great Falls. Before the members separated, they unanimously agreed to present the claims of the company to the legislatures of Maryland and Virginia for an extension of time to complete the navigation of the river, and agreed upon the following petition to be presented upon the opening of the sessions:—

To the Honorable the General Assemblies
of Virginia and Maryland.

The humble petition of the President and Directors of the Potomac Company in behalf of the said company, showeth:

That in and by the acts of the said assemblies for opening and extending the navigation of the Potomac River, it is provided and enacted, that in case the said company should not begin the work mentioned in the said act, within one year after the company should be formed, or if the navigation should not be made and improved between the Great Falls and Fort Cumberland in the manner therein before mentioned, within three years after the said company should be formed, then the said company should not be entitled to any benefit, privileges, or advantage under the said act.

That your petitioners conceive the intention of the legislatures in limiting the company to three years after the formation, for making and improving the navigation between the Great Falls and

Fort Cumberland, was to prevent any unnecessary delay in executing the work, and on the presumption that the time allowed was fully sufficient to effect it in the common and usual course of the seasons.

That the said company have entered on the work within the time limited, and prosecuted the same at great expense with unremitted assiduity, with such prospects of success that they hoped and expected to complete the whole navigation within the ten years allowed, but that the latter part of the summer and the fall of seventeen hundred and eighty-five were so unfavorable, that the hands employed in the bed of the river above the Great Falls were often drove from their work by rises of the water, and frequently kept out for several days together, so that the work could not proceed as was wished and expected. And the last summer hath proved so very rainy that the water has constantly kept up too high to permit any work to be done in the bed of the river, though the company retained a considerable number of men in their service through the whole of the last winter, with the view of being prepared to enter on the work about the twentieth day of June, the time that the water is generally low enough for such purpose, and thus by extraordinary exertion to retrieve the unavoidable loss of time in the preceding year.

Your petitioners therefore in behalf of the said company pray, "that acts of the said Assemblies may be passed whereby the said company may be indulged with time till the seventeenth day of November, seventeen hundred and ninety, or such other time as to your houses shall seem reasonable for making and improving the navigation between the Great Falls and Fort Cumberland."

This petition was submitted to the consideration of the meeting of the Board on the 2d day of October by the President of the company. It was unanimously adopted, and a committee was selected to proceed to Richmond and to Annapolis to present it to the legislatures as soon as they should be in session.

Upon its presentation by the committee, the General Assemblies promptly acted upon it, and authorized the extension of the time prayed for opening and extending the navigation of the Potomac. The preamble to this supplemental act declares, that "Whereas the two last summers have been so unfavorable to the work of making and improving the navigation above the Great Falls in the Potomac River, that the same cannot probably be perfected within the three years limited and allowed by the act for establishing a company for opening and extending the navigation of the River Potomac," and therefore granted the prayer of the petitioners, allowing until the seventeenth day of November, 1790, to complete the improvement.

The appointment of Mr. Richardson Stewart as the principal Assistant Superintendent, but with powers and a discretion conferred upon the General Superintendent, was not regarded by Mr. Rumsey with entire complacency and satisfaction.

The experience and knowledge of the construction of machinery, with the high personal character he possessed, pointed out Mr. Stewart as a very suitable individual to be engaged in the service of the company. At this time the importance of the use of machinery to raise the large boulders imbedded in the channel of the river, was beginning to be estimated, and no one was known better calculated to accomplish this purpose.

A short time after the appointment of Mr. Stewart, it was evident that Mr. Rumsey was becoming dissatisfied, and on several occasions evinced a disposition to impair the confidence of the Board in his skill and judgment and in the management of the important interest which was committed to his hands. A feeling allied to jealousy, and perhaps envy, so controlled him, that he retired from the service of the company under the plea of the incompetency, ignorance, and want of truth on the part of the newly appointed superintendent, and immediately prepared a list of charges against him, which he presented in person to the Board.

They were read by the clerk as follows:—

1st. The incapacity of the said manager for carrying on the great business of opening the River Potomac, his want of competent knowledge in mechanics, viz: in building four machines at a great expense for raising stone, none of which answered the purpose.

2d. The said manager's want of truth and candor in causing the overseers to have buried one of the said machines on the arrival of General Washington, that his ignorance might not come to the knowledge of the President and Directors, or accounting for the money so uselessly expended.

3d. The fifth machine he erected was still insufficient for the purpose intended, and did not succeed until materially amended by the late manager James Rumsey, notwithstanding he had disobeyed the orders of the said Rumsey before in constructing a machine for the above purpose, and to conceal his own misconduct had endeavored to ridicule the said machine to the overseers by putting it up before it was finished as planned by the said Rumsey, by which conduct not less than sixty dollars were entirely wasted.

4th. The said manager being unworthy of confidence by numerous misrepresentations to the President and Directors, especially the rock joining the canal (a place sufficiently known to the said Stewart and Directors without further description here), *first* by greatly approving it, and then concealing that approbation from Gen. Washington, Col. Gilpin, and Col. ———, and his extreme ignorance in intending but one wall (as he informed the late manager James Rumsey), which he himself had staked off on the inside of the canal, instead of the outside thereof, which all engineers will condemn.

5th. The said manager did greatly retard the operations by frequently ordering the people from the works the overseers had put them at, declaring it was wrong, and setting them to work at other places without any reason therefor, especially telling one of the overseers who convinced him he was wrong, that it was to keep up his dignity.

6th. That the said manager did greatly injure the said work, by introducing very improper persons as overseers, especially Owen Dolly, whose bad conduct even he was so ashamed of that he endeavored to hide it from the President and Directors by denying he ever acted as an overseer, thereby adding *falsity to fault*, and ——— Knox, who is now in Fairfax jail committed for forgery.

7th. That the said manager was very severe, not to say cruel, to the servants, which was not only very detrimental to those on the spot, but the rumors thereof reaching the neighborhood many persons coming to hire at the works were deterred and returned. That his misconduct has obliged Leonard Jamison and Joshua Crow, two overseers of unexceptionable good character, to leave the works, and has declared that old convicts make the best overseers, as themselves know what it is to be whipped.

8th. That the said manager, by declaring that officers of justice should not serve any process at the works, thereby encouraged the people under his command to depredate upon the neighboring inhabitants and destroy their stocks, and by his cruelty and bad behavior to individuals prevented necessaries being brought, especially his ordering a servant to spit in the face of Thomas Moxley, an inoffensive old man, and causing another servant to burn Michael Barnet with a hot iron without reason, which unworthy office the servant performed with such reluctance, that the manager, to compel it, was obliged to have recourse to blows, the injured person and beaten servant equally and justly complaining of such unparalleled wrongs.

9th. That when James Rumsey, the late manager, endeavored to compose the differences that had arisen between the people at the works and the neighborhood, in his absence the said Stewart endeavored to keep up the animosity by blaming the neighbors to the late manager, and exculpating the servants before the magistrates, and that upon all occasions in his power would insinuate against the late manager, repeating some things untrue, by concealing others, and in particular once before two of the Directors (wishing to saddle the late manager with the disorders which had happened in his absence) asserted, that he never saw a set of better behaved men, or men under better discipline, in his life, than the people were at the works on the arrival of the said Rumsey.

10th. That much injury has accrued to the company and the work much retarded by the fears of the country people occasioned by the manager's connivance at or occasioning of the ill treatment which too many persons had received, whom business or curiosity had induced to visit the works, insomuch that one of the contractors to feed the people (Col. Dark), since the appointment of Stewart cannot get wagoners or stock drivers to convey the provisions to the works, unless he will send one of his sons to protect them.

(Signed) JAMES RUMSEY.

August 4, 1786.

A copy of these charges were placed in the hands of the President and Directors of the company by Mr. Rumsey on the 4th of September, and had been duly considered, and witnesses examined, and the Board were prepared, the 3d of October, to submit their opinion of the matters in controversy. All the members were present, and also Mr. Rumsey and Mr. Stewart.

The President requested the clerk to read the opinion as follows:—

The Board having heard the charges aforesaid exhibited by Mr. James Rumsey, and the testimony adduced in support of them, and having maturely considered the testimony in support of them, are of opinion:—

On the 1st. Previous to the first appointment, the President and Directors took the measures they thought most likely to give them an opportunity of employing managers who had experience in works of the nature of that in contemplation, but as no person offered who had practical knowledge in such business, Mr. Rumsey was appointed, and continued as principal till his resignation, on which event the Board, under all circumstances, advanced the present to the place of the late manager without any endeavors on the part of Mr. Stewart to impress on the Board an idea of his competency to the work, and in general he has not fallen short of their expectations in its progress. The defect alleged in the four machines for raising stone was so easily remedied by a small addition, that the Board do not consider those machines as any evidence of Mr. Stewart's want of mechanical knowledge.

2d. It appears to the Board that no order was given by Mr. Stewart to have one of the machines buried, and that the part of the work concealed has been since made use of, and that Mr. Stewart's concealment of a part of it was not from any reprehensible motive, and that on the whole of the evidence this seems to be a frivolous charge.

3d. The inference in which this charge consists is unsupported.

4th. No misrepresentations having been made to the President and Directors, the first part of the charge is unfounded, and no evidence appears to support the remaining part of it.

5th.. It does not appear to the Board that Mr. Stewart used any severities that the necessity of the case did not require, and that Mr. Jamison and Mr. Crow having left the works should not be imputed to any misconduct in Mr. Stewart.

8th. The first part of the charge is unsupported by evidence, but that facts within the knowledge of the Board are in contradiction to it. With respect to Moxley, the evidence proves the order to have been given, but not executed, and that there must have been some misconception, as Mr. Stewart and he were on friendly terms and no provocation given. With respect to Barnet, the charge is proved, and that in this Mr. Stewart acted with an impropriety the Board disapproves of.

9th. The charge of Mr. Stewart endeavoring to keep up the animosity between the people at the works and the neighborhood, is not proved. His conduct before the magistrates from the information of one of them, appears to this Board to be proper and commendable; and the Board, nor any member of it, can recollect any conversation or insinuation of Mr. Stewart's, which had any tendency to lessen the late manager in their opinion.

10th. That the fears of the people of the neighborhood to visit the works have prevented that confidence and free intercourse which is desirable is too true, but the Board do not believe that Mr. Stewart hath given just cause for those fears. The Board have taken every means in their power to employ laborers and workmen who they expected would be the most easily governed, but their endeavors have been ineffectual. They have been reduced to the necessity either to let the work stand, or of purchasing servants and hiring such as have offered, amongst whom many have proved to be of very bad morals and turbulent dispositions. And this Board are of opinion that the fears of the country people have originated in the ill conduct of the people necessarily employed in the works, and have been widened by exaggeration. The Board are of opinion that Mr. Stewart, from several instances of his conduct, hath exerted himself to preserve regularity and order, and have a confidence that his conduct and that of all the company's officers will be calculated to this end, without which they can as little merit and expect the approbation of this Board.

During the past few months the number of hands in the service of the company was materially diminished, and as the present season was most favorable to the prosecution of the work, the Secretary was authorized to advertise for negroes to be hired on the same terms they were engaged the preceding year.

The managers were also directed to retain such of the hands as they might judge necessary, at monthly wages between the 12th day of November and the 12th day of April next, not exceeding 32*s.* sterling per month for common hands, nor 40*s.* sterling for prime hands, with the usual ration except spirits, and with such reasonable allowance of spirits as the manager may from time to time think proper, but shall not suffer rations to be issued to those who do not work, except in cases of necessity, and then to be charged to and deducted from the pay of the persons who receive them, unless in the few instances where the circumstances and merit of the man may claim such assistance, of which the Board expect account or information from time to time, to determine whether the provisions and money of the company are frugally expended.

Accounts amounting to £582 12*s.* 6*d.* were presented and passed at this meeting of the Board.

It was for some time apparent that unless extraordinary measures were adopted to compel subscribers to pay the dividends that were called in by resolution of the President and Board, the funds in the treasury would be insufficient to the employment of the force that was necessary to secure the earliest completion of the enterprise. The delinquent stockholders were several times addressed on the subject, and, with few exceptions, failed compliance with the demands of the company. Five months had nearly elapsed, and the funds were gradually diminishing, and without the prospect of replenishment. In consequence of this condition of the pecuniary affairs of the company, the President deemed it his duty to call a special meeting of the Board.

This meeting was held at Alexandria on Wednesday, the 3d day of January, 1787.

Present, GEORGE WASHINGTON, *President.*

JOHN FITZGERALD, Esq., GEORGE GILPIN, Esq., *Directors.*

The President then briefly stated the circumstances which induced him to call this meeting, the funds in the treasury were nearly exhausted, and it was a matter of much importance to the success of the enterprise, to continue the present force in the service of the company, but which could not be done, unless some measures were adopted to compel delinquent stockholders to pay the assessments upon the shares, in obedience to the Resolution of the Board in August last. He therefore earnestly invited deliberation and efficient action on the subject. After some conversation, and the interchange of views, it was ordered that a notification be directed to the subscribers in the words following, viz:—

BY THE PRESIDENT AND DIRECTORS
OF THE POTOMAC COMPANY:

Notice is hereby given to such of the subscribers for shares in the company, as are delinquents in making the payments heretofore called for by the Board, that unless the payment first called for, of 5 per cent., and the second, of 2½ per cent., on each share, are made to the Treasurer by the first of March next, the third, of 10 per cent., by the first of April next, and the fourth, of 10 per cent., by the first of May next, they will proceed to make immediate sale of the shares, agreeably to law. And for the information of such persons as have not made themselves acquainted with the directions of the law in this case, the Board think proper to inform them that if such sale does not produce the full sum ordered and directed to be advanced, as aforesaid, with the incidental charges, the said President and Directors, or a majority of them, may, in the name of the company, sue for, and recover the balance, by action of debtor on the case, and the said purchaser or purchasers shall be subject to the same rules and regulations as if the said sale and conveyance had been made by the original proprietor. And it is expected that those who have it in their power, will make their payments as early as possible, that the Board may be enabled to proceed in the work with new vigor.

By order of the Board,

(Signed) J. POTTS, Jr.,

Secretary.

This notice did not produce the effect desired or expected; a few of the proprietors paid into the hands of the Treasurer the first and second dividends within the time specified, but a large majority continued delinquent; and on the 3d day of April, 1787, the following advertisement was ordered to be published:—

BY THE PRESIDENT AND DIRECTORS
OF THE POTOMAC COMPANY:

Notice is hereby given, that in the pursuance of the power and authority vested in them by the act for opening and extending the navigation of the Potomac River, forty-six shares in the said company will be sold at auction, at the court-house, in Alexandria, in the State of Virginia, on Monday the fourteenth day of May next, at 11 o'clock in the forenoon, and nine shares, in the said company, will be sold at Shuter's tavern, in Georgetown, in the State of Maryland, on Monday the twenty-first day of May next, at 11 o'clock in the forenoon, they being the shares of such of the proprietors as are delinquents in making the first and second payments on their respective shares which have been heretofore called for by the Board.

By order of the Board,

J. POTTS, Jr.,

Secretary.

Upon the day of sale, the Directors proceeded to the court-house, in Alexandria, to give such information to bidders, in relation to the stock to be offered, as they might desire.

The novelty of the occasion drew thither a number of persons. The auctioneer was unsuccessful; no bids were made, and the Directors present suspended the proceedings, and the following notice was directed to be published:—

BY THE PRESIDENT AND DIRECTORS
OF THE POTOMAC COMPANY:

Notice is hereby given that in pursuance of the power and authority vested in them by the act for opening and extending the navigation of the Potomac River, all the shares in the company on which the requisitions heretofore made by the Board have not been paid will be offered for sale at auction; such of them as were subscribed for in the State of Virginia, at the court-house in Alexandria, on Tuesday the 26th day of June next, between the hours of eleven and twelve ; and such of them as were subscribed for in Maryland, at Shuter's tavern, in Georgetown, on the day following.

On the day specified in the above notice, the shares in the company were offered for sale at Georgetown, and was attended with the same result as that previously at Alexandria. No bids were made, but many of the delinquent stockholders having made payment of their arrearages, and others having given assurances of paying within a short time, the Board deemed it advisable to indulge the delinquent proprietors of shares until the 6th day of August next; and gave public notice that if the several payments heretofore called for, shall not have been made by the day stated, the shares will *positively* be sold.

The 6th of August being the day appointed by law for holding the general meeting, all the shareholders were earnestly requested to attend, either in person or by proxy, in order that some efficient measures be adopted, to place the affairs of the company in a condition to prosecute the work with energy and force.

It was also ordered that the further sum of 6 per cent. be paid on each share on or before the fifteenth day of August next, and the Secretary to give an order on the Treasurer for £300 sterling in favor of Col. Dark in account.

On the day appointed for holding the general meeting at Georgetown and for disposing of the shares of the members delinquent in making the payments, called for by previous orders of the Board, there being but a few of the proprietors in attendance, the business intended to be brought before it was postponed to the 22d day of October, to which day the annual election was also deferred.

The general meeting was held in pursuance to the last adjournment, and was organized by the appointment of Daniel Carroll, Esq., Chairman, and John Potts, Jr., Esq., acting as Clerk.

A list of members present being taken, and also of the proxies, it appeared that one hundred and forty-four shares were represented.

The meeting then proceeded to the election of President and Directors for the ensuing year. On counting the ballots, it was determined that the following named gentlemen were unanimously elected:—

General George Washington, *President.*

Thos. Johnston, Thos. S. Lee, John Fitzgerald, George Gilpin, Esqrs., *Directors.*

It was then resolved that a committee be appointed to receive and examine the report and proceedings of the President and Directors for the last year, to consist of six members, three of whom to be a quorum, to act and make a report of the same to the next general meeting. Wm. Herbert, Wm. Hunter

Jr., Josiah Wasson, Saml. Davidson, Bernard O'Neale, and Wm. Deakins, Jr., were accordingly appointed.

It was also resolved that the President and Directors be requested to apply to the Legislatures of Virginia and Maryland to authorize them to recover in a summary manner the sums of money called for from time to time, from such of the proprietors as are delinquent in making their payments.

The funds of the company were rapidly diminishing. For some time extraordinary drafts were made upon the treasury, on account of the increased number of hands employed at the Great Falls, and in the construction of boats and the machinery for raising rocks from the bed of the river. The efforts of the officers to induce the stockholders yet delinquent in the payment of their arrearages, to make remittances, were so far unavailing, and the Board found it necessary at its next meeting to anticipate by a specified time the completion of sufficient part of the navigation to give encouragement to the proprietors, and insure remittances to the Treasurer. A variety of causes had operated to check the progress of the improvement thus far, notwithstanding the unceasing efforts of the President and Directors of the company. Many of the difficulties that were encountered were unavoidable, and could only be overcome by a patient forbearance, a steady perseverance, and a continued confidence in the final success of the enterprise.

The President called a meeting of the Board at the mouth of the Shenandoah, on 2d day of June, 1788.

Present: Gen. GEORGE WASHINGTON, *President.*

THOS. S. LEE, GEORGE GILPIN, THOS. JOHNSTON, *Directors.*

In consequence of the removal of Mr. Potts, the Secretary of the Company, to Philadelphia, Mr. Hartshorne, the Treasurer, was requested to make entries of the proceedings of the meeting, and to act in this capacity until a suitable person could be chosen as secretary.

Mr. Hartshorne presented a brief but interesting statement of the amount of funds in the treasury; this statement formed the basis upon which proceedings of the meeting were founded.

After much conversation and the interchange of views, it was unanimously admitted that the current expenses of the organization might be lessened without jeopardizing the progress of the work, or the assurance to the stockholders that, by the approaching season, the navigation would be so far perfected as to permit the passage of loaded boats from the reach above the Seneca Falls to tide-water. It was also determined that as soon as the state of the water was sufficiently low in July to work to advantage in the channel of the Shenandoah Falls, the number of hands would be augmented at that point to remove its obstructions as speedily as possible.

With these encouraging proceedings, the Board

cherished the hope of receiving early and efficient pecuniary relief from the proprietors, and which would enable them to do more than they had promised to them with the means in their possession.

The first step towards abridging the expenses of the company was the reduction of the number of managers to one for the entire line, and specially fixing his salary—and to allow no extra or contingent accounts to any officer of the company. The principal manager was allowed £25, in addition to his annual salary, per year in future, to indemnify him for the expenses he may incur by the visits of the President and Directors, and strangers travelling, and other personal expenses.

Mr. Richardson Stewart, who had been in the employment of the company as manager since March, 1786, was removed for reasons relative to the interest of the company, and the assistant, Mr. James Smith, was appointed principal manager in his place.

For some time past the conduct of Mr. Stewart had created dissatisfaction among the subordinate officers of the company on the river, and sundry charges of a serious nature were brought against him, which were submitted to the Board to be investigated. Mr. Stewart's absence prevented the examination then taking place, and the matter was postponed with the verbal understanding that in the event of the charges not being withdrawn, they would, upon application, be called up at a future day.

In the mean time, however, the President and Board addressed the following letter to Mr. Stewart:—

SHENANDOAH, June 2, 1788.

MR. RICHARDSON STEWART:

We met to day by appointment to hear the charges against you, but could not with propriety go into an examination of witnesses in your absence, which, however to be regretted, we believe involuntary. On a general view of the situation of the company's affairs, being of opinion that the present fund or prospects will not warrant our continuing two managers, we have come to the inclosed resolution. It is with reluctance we found ourselves under the necessity to make arrangements which, at this point of time, may possibly be thought, by your enemies, to be occasioned by the charges against you, but it has proceeded solely from our duty and inclination to promote the company's interest, without being influenced in any degree by facts alleged and not examined into. The preference given to Mr. Smith is on different principles, and we expect cannot surprise you or hurt your feelings. We request on the expiration of your present year, you will deliver up the property of the company under your care into his hands.

We are, sir,

Your very humble servants,

G. W.
T. J.
T. L.
G.

Mr. Stewart not being present, but, as the Board have reason to believe, necessarily absent, attending a law suit, the President and Directors decline going into an examination of witnesses in support of the charges exhibited against him.

And it is also ordered, that no overseer be retained in the company's service at higher wages than four pounds per month.

The subject of replenishing the funds in the treasury still pressed itself upon the attention of the Board; and it was decided that a communication be addressed to every delinquent proprietor, to pay all the arrearages on his stock; and also to inclose therewith copies of all notices of previous and existing delinquencies heretofore published, with the following explicit order:—

Therefore, it is ordered that each and every stockholder or proprietor of any share or shares in the said company, pay to Mr. Hartshorne, Treasurer of said company, all such sums of money as now remain due from them respectively, on account of the foregoing orders, or any of them, on or before the 1st day of October next.

Geo. Washington, *P.*
Geo. Gilpin,
John Fitzgerald.

The next annual meeting of the stockholders was held in Alexandria, on the 4th day of August, 1788, and was organized by appointing Philip Richard Fendall, Esq., Chairman, and William Hartshorne, Esq., Secretary.

The report of the President and Directors for the preceding year was presented and read; and from which it appeared that in consequence of the unusual height of the water in the river, during the past spring and summer, the progress of the improvement was greatly retarded, but hopes were expressed that an ordinary favorable season would secure the removal of the obstacles in the channel of navigation from the Great Falls to Cumberland, sufficiently, by the 1st of November ensuing, to permit loaded boats to run between these points.

It also appeared that the several sums of money paid into the treasury since the last meeting of the company amounted to £2,990 2*s.* 2*d.* sterling, which being added to the amount previously paid, made an aggregate of £13,719 18*s.* 8*d.* sterling.

A committee, composed of Col. Hooe, Col. John Allison, and Mr. William Lowry, was appointed by the Chairman, to examine the accounts of the Treasurer. This examination having been made, the committee reported that the accounts were fairly stated, and exhibited a balance in hand of £169 10*s.* 6*d.* Virginia currency.

Although General Washington earnestly desired to withdraw from the position he had occupied in the Potomac Company from the day of its organization, the stockholders were unwilling to permit him to retire from the Presidency and its active duties, without a manifestation of their regard and gratitude, and an expression of the value of his services, and of their appreciation of the zeal and ability he had devoted to their interests.

This was the memorable year preceding the change

of the government from a confederation to a constitutional form. The subject had already, to a very great extent, excited the public attention, but it was not a question "*Whom shall we choose as the first President of the United States?*"

For the Chief Magistrate of the nation, all eyes were directed to the illustrious Washington. He had led the country in triumph through the struggles of the revolutionary war, secured to it the blessings of civil and religious liberty, and had deeply implanted himself in the hearts of the American people by his own disinterested example in the holy cause of freedom, a love of country, and an uncontrollable repugnance to tyranny and oppression. And every American bosom, overflowing with gratitude for his patriotic services, and unspotted purity of character, was ready with one outburst of acclamation to place him in the chair of the Chief Executive of the nation.

With this unanimity of national sentiment, the Directors and proprietors of the Potomac Company cordially united, however painful would be the separation of their official relation to the beloved Washington; the public good demanded the sacrifice, and they were prepared to yield to its necessity with becoming grace and resignation.

This was the day for the annual election, and General Washington, having been earnestly entreated, yielded to the wishes of the proprietors to allow his name to remain as a Director of the company. Yet still more to distinguish the love and admiration the members of the company cherished for the man, who was "first in war, first in peace, and first in the hearts of his countrymen," they postponed the election of President of the Potomac Company to the year 1789. This was a compliment delicately and gracefully bestowed; and could not have been more justly deserved. It was fully appreciated by General Washington.

Before the adjournment, Mr. Richardson Stewart presented an account, from Doctor Tiffin, of eight pounds, Virginia currency, for curing Patrick Todd of a wound he had received while in the service of the company, and which the treasurer was authorized to pay.

And also, on motion of Col. Fitzgerald, seconded by Mr. Dulany, a committee was appointed, composed of Col. Hooe, Col. John Allison, and Mr. Lowry, from Virginia, and Col. Deakins, Mr. Stoddart, and Mr. O'Neale, of Maryland, or any one of these gentlemen, from each State, to examine the accounts of the ensuing year, and to make their report to the next annual meeting, which was ordered to be held at Georgetown, on the 3d day of August, 1789.

The miscellaneous business before the company having been concluded, the chairman notified the proprietors present, and the proxies, that this was the day specified by the charter, for holding the annual election for President and Directors, and requested them to prepare their ballots; which being cast and counted, the following named gentlemen were found to be unanimously elected: General Washington, Thomas Sim Lee, John Fitzgerald, and George Gilpin, Esqrs.

For cause not stated in the record of the proceedings of the proprietors, or of the Directors, no meetings were held previous to the annual appointment for the 3d day of March, 1789.

On this day, members of the company and proxies, amounting to a representation of one hundred and eight shares, attended at Georgetown—a sufficient number for the transaction of business.

Robert Peter, Esq., was unanimously appointed Chairman of the meeting.

A committee, as usual, was appointed to examine the accounts of the Treasurer, and report thereon. The Chairman appointed Robert T. Hooe, George Digges, and Marisham Waring.

The meeting then proceeded to the election of a President and Directors. The following gentlemen were chosen:—

THOMAS JOHNSTON, *President.*

GEORGE GILPIN, JOHN FITZGERALD, THOS. S. LEE, NOTLEY YOUNG, *Directors.*

After the retirement of General Washington from the Presidency of the company in 1788, the zeal and energies of many of its proprietors greatly relaxed, and discouragements ensued. The original cost of the improvement, and the time specified for its completion, both failing to be realized, it was for some time doubtful whether the enterprise would not be entirely abandoned.

The result, however, of discussions on this subject, was favorable to the prosecution of the improvement. The original estimate of the engineers and mechanics that were selected to make the surveys and calculate the cost of the improvement, the boats, machinery, &c., was $250,000, and three years was allowed as the time for its expenditure, and for the completion of the navigation.

But long before the expiration of the time specified by the charter, it was evident, from the exhausted condition of the finances, and the little progress that was made in the work, that more money and time would be required. Applications were accordingly presented to the Legislatures of Virginia and Maryland for an extension of three years beyond the existing term. The extension was obtained, yet was still insufficient.

In looking over the record of the proceedings of the General Assemblies of Virginia and Maryland, relative to the company, it will be seen that ten amendatory acts were passed at different periods between the sessions of 1786, when the first application for an extension was granted, and the year 1820.

Although insufficient, these repeated applications

to the legislatures, and the readiness with which they were granted, evince the continued and unabated confidence that was entertained in its final success, and the accomplishment of the earnest hopes and expectations of the proprietors.

By this time, however, the successful prosecution of the construction of the *Great Erie Canal* in the State of New York, attracted attention to an extraordinary degree. That great work, undertaken by a State, unaided by the general government, was well calculated to attract and excite the admiration and astonishment of the country. Many proprietors of the Potomac Company at length despairing of accomplishing the purpose of the charter, "*the improvement of the navigation of the Potomac River, from tide-water to the highest point practicable, and a highway across the portage to the waters of the Ohio*," changed their views as to this particular plan, and with the example of a continuous canal of 365 miles in length being undertaken by a sister State, to encourage them, they applied to the General Assembly of Virginia to authorize the Board of Public Works to appoint an engineer "to examine the waters of the Potomac above the upper line of the District of Columbia, and to explore the country between the Potomac and Ohio, on the one side, and the Potomac and Rappahannock on the other, with a view to ascertain and report upon the practicability of affording a communication by canal between these three rivers."

Thus, after a protracted existence of thirty-six years, and an expenditure of $729,380, in the prosecution of the enterprise of the Potomac Company, it was determined to relinquish the original plan of improvement, and adopt another of a character supposed to be more feasible.

The Board of Public Works responded favorably to the resolution of the General Assembly, and commissioners were appointed, the examinations made, and their report was communicated by the Governor to the General Assembly.

The report affirms the practicability of the construction of a continuous canal, and upon this interesting fact being communicated, the Legislatures of Virginia and Maryland concurrently appointed a joint commission to examine the affairs of the Potomac Company, the state of the navigation of the River Potomac, its susceptibility of improvement, and to make report whether the said company had complied with its charter granted by the two States, and its ability to comply within a reasonable time; and whether any, or what aid should be given to the said company, and what would be the best means of effecting an improvement in the navigation of the said river.

In July, 1822, the commission entered upon the discharge of its duties, and after a very laborious investigation of its affairs, reported, in effect, "that the affairs of the Potomac Company had failed to comply with the terms and conditions of the charter; that there was no reasonable ground to expect that they would be able to effect the objects of their incorporation; that they had not only expended their capital stock and the tolls received, with the exception of a small dividend of five dollars and fifty cents on each share declared in 1802, but had incurred a heavy debt which their resources would never enable them to discharge; that the floods and freshets nevertheless gave the only navigation that was enjoyed; that the whole time when produce and goods could be stream borne on the Potomac in the course of an entire year, did not exceed forty-five days; that it would be imprudent and inexpedient to give further aid to the Potomac Company."

Thus terminated the existence of this time honored enterprise, and from its termination originated THE CHESAPEAKE AND OHIO CANAL COMPANY.

PART III.

When General Washington divested himself of the cares and responsibilities of the command of the army, and retired from the public service, he engaged extensively in correspondence with some of the most distinguished men who had shared with him the toils and perils of the war, on the several subjects of national concern, and which the successful termination of the Revolution naturally produced. These subjects were canvassed with the greatest candor and frankness; and all his letters breathe with the most fervent love for the principles of good government, and the *union* of the States. His sagacious and well-balanced mind, comprehending, as it were, by intuition, the difficulties that might arise in the progress of the confederacy, and in forming a more perfect *union*, failed not to appreciate the importance of the establishment of a *system* of internal improvement. He regarded it as the most valuable auxiliary to the political bonds which connected together the integral and extreme parts of the whole country, and in view of this object he contemplated the consummation of the favorite project of his early years, with more than ordinary interest.

Not long after his retirement, he renewed, with unabated zeal and earnestness, the *Potomac enterprise*, *a project*, though unaccomplished, which unquestionably was the basis and introduction of that important measure of national policy subsequently *adopted*, and styled the *system of internal improvement*, and from which the trade and business of the country derived incalculable benefits; and to which the West particularly is indebted for its rapid growth in population and commercial prosperity.

Although the extracts from his private correspondence which follow have not an exclusive reference to the single *project* which forms the basis of this compilation, they are deemed essential to the completeness of its monographic character, and add vastly to its interest.

One of the first letters after his return to Mount Vernon was addressed to Marquis LAFAYETTE, dated 1st of Feb. 1784. The style and language of this letter are characteristic of the *heart* and *mind* of the "FATHER OF HIS COUNTRY," and form an appropriate introduction to this part of the compilation. It is therefore given nearly entire.

At length, my dear Marquis, I am become a private citizen on the banks of the Potomac, and under the shadow of my own vine and fig-tree, far from the bustle of a camp and the busy scenes of a public life, I am solacing myself with these tranquil enjoyments of which the soldier who is ever in pursuit of fame; the statesman whose watchful days and sleepless nights are spent in devising schemes to promote the welfare of his own, perhaps the ruin of other countries, as if the globe was insufficient for us all; and the courtier, who is always watching the countenance of his prince, in hopes of catching a gracious smile, can have very little conception. I have not only retired from all public employments, but I am retired within myself, and shall be able to view the solitary walk, and tread the paths of private life with a heart-felt satisfaction. Envious of none, I am determined to be pleased with all. And this, my dear friend, being the order for my march, I will move gently down the stream of life, until I sleep with my fathers.

The following extracts of two letters are equally characteristic. The first letter is addressed to Major General KNOX, and dated the 20th February 1784.

I am just beginning to experience that ease and freedom from public cares, which, however desirable, takes some time to realize; for, strange as it may seem, it is nevertheless true, that it was not till lately I could get the better of my usual custom of ruminating as soon as I waked in the morning on the business of the ensuing day; and of my surprise at finding, after revolving many things in my mind, that I was no longer a public man, nor had anything to do with public transactions.

I feel now, however, as I conceive a wearied traveller must do, after treading many a painful step with a heavy burthen on his shoulders, is eased of the latter, having reached the haven to which all the former were directed, and from his house-top is looking back, and tracing with an eager eye the meanders by which he escaped the quicksands and mires which lay in his way; and into which none but the all-powerful guide and dispenser of human events could have prevented his falling.

The other is an extract of a letter to the Marchioness De Lafayette, dated April 4th, 1784.

Freed from the clangor of arms and the bustle of a camp, from the cares of public employment and the responsibilities of office, I am now enjoying domestic ease under the shadow of my own vine and my own fig-tree; and in a small villa, with the implements of husbandry and lambkins around me, I expect to glide gently down the stream of life, till I am entombed in the mansion of my fathers.

Shortly after his return from his tour to the West, in the autumn of 1784, which was principally undertaken to possess himself of a personal knowledge of the character of the country lying between the head-waters of the Potomac and the tributaries of the Ohio River, and enable him to estimate with greater accuracy the difficulties attending the construction of a public highway across the gorge of the mountain, he addressed a long letter to Benjamin Harrison, Governor of Virginia.

This letter is dated "Mount Vernon, Oct. 10th,

1784, and contains such a series of interesting facts, strengthening the propriety of his suggestion, relative to the importance of opening a communication between the East and the West, that I cannot forbear drawing largely from it—to abridge the extract would greatly impair its perspicuity and comprehensiveness, and the force with which the scheme is recommended.

On my return from the western country, a few days ago, I had the pleasure to receive your favor of the 17th ultimo. It has always been my intention to pay my respects to you, before the chance of another early and hard winter should make a warm fire-side too comfortable to be relinquished. And I shall feel the additional pleasure in offering this tribute of friendship and respect to you, by having the company of the Marquis De Lafayette, when he shall have revisited this place from his eastern tour, now every day to be expected.

I shall take the liberty now, my dear sir, to suggest a matter which would (if I am not too short-sighted a politician) mark your administration as an important era in the annals of this country, if it should be recommended by you and adopted by the Assembly.

It has long been my decided opinion, that the shortest, easiest, and least expensive communication with the invaluable and extensive country back of us, would be by one or both of the rivers of this State, which have their sources in the Appalachian Mountains. Nor am I singular in this opinion. Evans, in his map and analysis of the Middle Colonies, which, considering the early period at which they were given to the public, are done with amazing exactness; and Hutchins, since, in his Topographical Description of the Western Country, a good part of which is from actual surveys, are decidedly of the same sentiments, as, indeed, are all others, who have had opportunities, and have been at the pains to investigate and consider the subject.

But that this may not now stand as mere matter of opinion and assertion, unsupported by facts (such, at least, as the best maps now extant, compared with the oral testimony which my opportunities in the course of the war have enabled me to obtain), I shall give you the different routes and distances from Detroit, by which all the trade of the northwestern parts of the united territory must pass; unless the Spaniards, contrary to their present policy, should engage part of it, or the British should attempt to force nature, by carrying the trade of the upper lakes by the River Utawas, into Canada, which I scarcely think they will or could effect. Taking Detroit, then (which is putting ourselves in as unfavorable a point of view as we can well be placed in, because it is upon the line of the British territory), as a point by which, as I have already observed, all that part of the trade must come, it appears from the statement inclosed, that the tide-waters of the State are nearer to it by one hundred and sixty-eight miles, than those of the River St. Lawrence, or than those of the Hudson at Albany, by one hundred and seventy-six miles.

Maryland stands upon similar ground with Virginia. Pennsylvania, although the Susquehanna is an unfriendly water, much impeded, it is said, with rocks and rapids, and nowhere communicating with those which lead to her capital, has it in contemplation to open a communication between Toby's Creek, which empties into the Alleghany River ninety-five miles above Fort Pitt, and the West Branch of the Susquehanna, and to cut a canal between the waters of the latter and the Schuylkill; the expense of which is easier to be conceived than estimated or described by me. A people, however, who are possessed of the spirit of commerce, who see, and who will pursue their advantages, may achieve almost anything. In the mean time, under the uncertainty of these undertakings, they are smoothing the roads, and paving the ways for the trade of the western world. That New York will do the same, as soon as the British garrisons are removed, which are at present insurmountable obstacles in their way, no person who knows the temper, genius, and policy of those people as well as I do, can harbor the smallest doubt.

Thus much with respect to rival States. Let me now take a short view of our own; and, being aware of the objections which are in the way, I will, in order to contrast them, enumerate them with the advantages.

The first and principal one is the *unfortunate jealousy* which ever has, and it is to be feared ever will prevail, lest one part of the State should obtain an advantage over the other parts, as if the benefits of the trade were not diffusive and beneficial to all. Then follows a train of difficulties, namely, that our people are already heavily taxed; that we have no money; that the advantages of this trade are remote; that the most direct route for it is through other States, over which we have no control; that the routes over which we have control are as distant as either of those which lead to Philadelphia, Albany, or Montreal; that a sufficient spirit of commerce does not pervade the citizens of this commonwealth; and that we are, in fact, doing for others what they ought to do for themselves.

Without going into the investigation of a question which has employed the pens of able politicians, namely, whether trade with foreigners is an advantage or disadvantage to a country, this State is a part of the confederated States, all of which have the spirit of it very strongly working within them, must adopt it, or submit to the evils arising therefrom without receiving its benefits. Common policy, therefore, points clearly and strongly to the propriety of our enjoying all the advantages which nature and our local situation afford us; and evinces clearly that unless the spirit could be totally eradicated in other States as well as in this, and every man be made to become either a cultivator of the land or a manufacturer of such articles as are prompted by necessity, such stimulus should be employed as will *force* this spirit, by showing to our countrymen the superior advantages we possess beyond others, and the importance of being upon an equal footing with our neighbors.

If this is fair reasoning, it ought to follow as a consequence, that we should do our part towards opening the communication for the fur and peltry trade of the lakes, and for the produce of the country which lies within, and which will, so soon as matters are settled with the Indians, and the terms on which Congress mean to dispose of the land found to be favorable, are announced, be settled faster than any other ever was, or any one would imagine. This, then, when considered in an interested point of view, is alone sufficient to excite our endeavors. But in my opinion, there is a political consideration for so doing, which is of still greater importance.

I need not remark to you, sir, that the flanks and rear of the United States are possessed by other powers, and formidable ones too; nor how necessary it is to apply the cement of interest to bind all parts of the Union together by indissoluble bonds, especially that part of it which lies immediately west of us, with the Middle States. For what ties, let me ask, should we have upon those people? How entirely unconnected with them shall we be, and what troubles may we not apprehend, if the Spaniards on their right, and Great Britain on their left, instead of throwing stumbling blocks in their way, as they now do, should hold out lures for their trade and alliance? What, when they get strength, which will be sooner than most people conceive (from the emigration of foreigners, who will have no particular predilection towards us, as well as from the removal of our own citizens), will be the consequence of their having formed close connections with both or either of those powers, in a commercial way, it needs not, in my opinion, the gift of prophecy to foretell.

The Western States (I speak now from my own observation) stand as it were upon a pivot. The touch of a feather would turn them any way. They have looked down the Mississippi until the Spaniards, very impolitically, I think, for themselves, threw difficulties in their way; and they looked that way for no other reason than because they could glide gently down the stream, without considering, perhaps, the difficulties of the voyage back again, and the time necessary to perform it in; and because they have no other means of coming to us but by long land transportations, and unimproved roads. These causes have hitherto checked the industry of the present settlers; for, except the demand for provisions, occasioned by the increase of population, and a little flour, which the necessities of the Spaniards compel them to buy, they have no incitements to labor. But smooth the road, and make easy the way for them, and then see what an influx of articles will be poured upon us; how amazingly our exports will be increased by them, and how amply we shall be compensated for any trouble and expense we may encounter to effect it.

A combination of circumstances makes the present conjunction more favorable for Virginia than for any other State in the Union, to fix these matters. The jealous and untoward disposition of the Spaniards, on one hand, and the private views of some individuals, coinciding with the general policy of the court of Great Britain on the other, to retain as long as possible the posts of Detroit, Niagara, and Oswego (which, though done under the letter of the treaty, is certainly an infraction of the spirit of it, and injurious to the Union), may be improved to the greatest advantage by the State, if she would open the avenues to the trade of that country, and embrace the present moment to establish it. It only wants a beginning. The western inhabitants would do their part towards its execution. Weak as they are, they would meet us at least half-way, rather than be driven into the arms of foreigners, or be made dependent upon them; which would eventually either bring on a separation of them from us, or a war between the United States and one or the other of those powers, most probably with the Spaniards.

The preliminary steps to the attainment of this great object would be attended with very little expense, and might, at the same time that it served to attract the attention of the western country, and convince the wavering inhabitants of our disposition to connect ourselves with them, and facilitate their commerce with us, be a means of removing those jealousies which otherwise might take place among ourselves.

These, in my opinion, are to appoint commissioners, who, from their situation, integrity, and abilities, can be under no suspicion of prejudice or predilection to one part more than to another. Let these commissioners make an actual survey of James River and the Potomac from tide-water to their respective sources; note with great accuracy the kind of navigation, and the obstructions, the distances from place to place, through their whole extent, and the nearest and best portage between these waters, and the streams capable of improvement, which run into the Ohio; traverse these in like manner to their junction with the Ohio, and with equal accuracy. The navigation of the Ohio being well known, they will have less to do in the examination of it; but nevertheless, let the sources and distances be taken to the mouth of the Muskingum, and up that river (notwithstanding it is in the ceded lands) to the carrying place to the Cayahoga; down the Cayahoga to Lake Erie; and thence to Detroit. Let them do the same with Big Beaver Creek; although part of it is in the State of Pennsylvania; and also with the Scioto. In a word, let the waters east and west of the Ohio, which invite our notice by their proximity and by the ease with which land transportation may be had between them and the Lakes on the one side, and the Rivers Potomac and James on the other, be explored, accurately delineated, and a correct and connected map of the whole be presented to the public. These things being done, I shall be mistaken if prejudice does not yield to facts, jealousy to candor, and, finally, if reason and nature, thus aided, do not dictate what is right and proper to be done.

In the meanwhile, if it should be thought that the lapse of time, which is necessary to effect this work, may be attended with injurious consequences, could not there be a sum of money granted towards opening the best, or, if it should be deemed more eligible, two of the nearest communications (one to the northward, and another to the southward), with the settlements to the westward, and an act be passed, if there should not appear a manifest disposition in the Assembly to make it a public undertaking, to incorporate and encourage private adventurers, if any should associate and solicit the same, for the purpose of extending the navigation of the Potomac or James River; and, in the former case, to request the concurrence of Maryland in the measure? It will appear from my statement of the different routes (and, as far as my means of information have extended, I have done it with the utmost candor), that all the produce of the settlements about Fort Pitt can be brought to Alexandria by the Youghiogheny in three hundred and four miles, whereof only thirty-one are land transportation; and by the Monongahela and Cheat Rivers in three hundred and sixty miles, twenty of which only are land carriage. Whereas, the common road from Fort Pitt to Philadelphia is three hundred and twenty miles, all land transportation; or four hundred and seventy-six miles, if the Ohio, Toby's Creek, Susquehanna and Schuylkill, are made use of for this purpose. How much of this is by land, I know not; but, from the nature of the country, it must be very considerable. How much the interest and the feelings of people thus circumstanced would be engaged to promote it, requires no illustration.

For my own part, I think it highly probable, that upon the strictest scrutiny, if the Falls of the Great Kenawha can be made navigable, or a short portage be had there, it will be found of equal importance and convenience to improve the navigation of both the James and Potomac. The latter, I am fully persuaded, affords the nearest communication with the Lakes; but James River may be more convenient for all the settlers below the mouth of the Great Kenawha, and for some distance perhaps above and west of it; for I have no expectation, that any part of the trade above the Falls of the Ohio will go down that river and the Mississippi, much less that the returns will ever come up them; or, upon trial, if it should be found that these rivers, from the before-mentioned Falls, will admit the descent of sea-vessels, in that case, and the navigation of the former becoming free, it is probable that both vessels and cargoes will be carried to foreign markets and sold; but the returns for them will never, in the natural course of things, ascend the long and rapid current of that river, which, with the Ohio to the Falls, in their meanderings, is little, if any, short of two thousand miles. Upon the whole, the object in my estimation is of vast commercial and political importance. In this light I think they will consider it, and regret if our conduct should give them cause that the present favorable moment to secure so great a blessing for them was neglected.

One thing more remains, which I had like to have forgotten, and that is, the supposed difficulty of obtaining a passage through the State of Pennsylvania. How an application to its legislature would be relished, in the first instance, I will not undertake to decide; but of one thing I am almost certain, such an application would place that body in a very delicate situation. There are in the State of Pennsylvania at least one hundred thousand souls west of the Laurel Hill, who are groaning under the inconveniences of a long land transportation. They are wishing, indeed they are looking for the improvement and extension of inland navigation; and, if this cannot be made easy for them to Philadelphia (at any rate it must be long), they will seek a mart elsewhere; the consequence of which would be, that the State, though contrary to the interests of its seaports, must submit to the loss of so much of its trade, or hazard not only the loss of the trade but the loss of the settlement also; for an opposition on the part of government to the extension of water transportation so consonant with the essential interests of a large body of people, or any extraordinary impositions upon the exports or imports to or from another State, would ultimately bring on a separation between its eastern and western settlements; towards which there is not wanting a disposition at this moment in that part of it beyond the mountains. I consider Rumsey's discovery for working boats against the stream, by mechanical power principally, as not only a very fortunate invention for these States, in general, but as one of those circumstances which have combined to render the present time favorable above all others for fixing, if we are disposed to avail ourselves of them, a large portion of the trade of the western country in the bosom of this State irrevocably.

Long as this letter is, I intended to have written a fuller and more digested one, upon this important subject; but have met with so many interruptions since my return home, as almost to have precluded my writing at all. What I now give is crude; but if you are in sentiment with me, I have said enough; if there is not an accordance of opinion, I have said too much; and all I pray in the latter case is, that you will do me the justice to believe my motives are pure, however erroneous my judgment may be in this matter, and that I am with the most perfect esteem and friendship,

Sir, yours, &c.

Not long after the memorials for the connection between the eastern and western sides of the Alleghany Mountains were presented to the Legislatures of Virginia and Maryland, General Washington felt it to be his duty to bring the subject, in a national form, before the Congress of the United States. Richard Henry Lee was President of that body. As preliminary to the adoption of any definite measures, looking directly to this union, by an internal communication, he earnestly invoked the wisdom and attention of Congress, to provide the means for an accurate survey of the western country between specified limits; and upon the result of this survey depended a more particular recommendation of his object to its favor and support. His letter to Mr. Lee, from which the following extract is taken, is dated—

MOUNT VERNON, December 14, 1784.

The Assemblies of Virginia and Maryland have now under consideration the extension of the inland navigation of the Rivers Potomac and James, and opening a communication between them and the western waters. They seem fully impressed with the political, as well as the commercial advantages, which would result from the accomplishment of these great objects; and I hope will embrace the present moment to put them in a train for execution. Would it not, at the same time, be worthy of the wisdom and attention of Congress, to have the western waters well explored, the navigation of them fully ascertained, accurately laid down, and a complete and perfect map made of the country; at least as far westwardly as the Miamies, running into the Ohio and Lake Erie, and to see how the waters of these communicate with the River St. Joseph, which empties into the Lake Michigan, and with the Wabash? For I cannot forbear observing that the Miami Village, in Hutchins' map, if it and the waters are laid down with accuracy, points to a very important post for the Union. The expense attending such an undertaking could not be great; the advantages would be unbounded; for sure I am, nature has made such a display of her bounties in those regions, that the more the country is explored the more it will rise in estimation, consequently the greater will the revenue be to the Union.

The project of improving the navigation of the Potomac River had for some time attracted attention both in Virginia and Maryland; and many of their most prominent citizens were earnestly engaged in advancing the interests of the enterprise. The only difficulty which seemed to present itself in its accomplishment, was the arrangement of details, to render it mutually satisfactory and advantageous to the parties—*two sovereign and independent States.* Their respective legislatures had already sufficiently responded to the public sentiment, to indicate the character of their future action, whenever the scheme would be formally submitted to them; and to settle the preliminaries on just and equitable principles. General Gates and General Washington were requested, on the part of Virginia, to visit Annapolis on a mission of consultation on the subject with the proper authorities of Maryland.

Immediately on their arrival in the ancient metropolis of Maryland, General Washington wrote to Marquis De Lafayette as follows:—

I am here with General Gates, at the request of the Assembly of Virginia, to fix matters with the Assembly of this State, respecting the extension of the inland navigation of the Potomac, and the communication between it and the western waters; and I hope a plan will be agreed upon to the mutual satisfaction of both States, and to the advantage of the Union at large.

The Legislature of Virginia manifested their appreciation of the great public services of General Washington, by the unanimous passage of an act of donation, vesting in him the exclusive interest in one hundred and fifty shares in the Potomac and James Rivers Navigation Companies. This act of gratitude expressed the universal sentiment of the people of the State, and placed upon these two enterprises the seal of confidence, not only in their practicability, but, when accomplished, as sources of revenue.

In reply to the letter from the Governor of the State, gracefully declining the acceptance of the proffered gift, General WASHINGTON remarks:—

It is not for me to decide by which my mind was most affected, upon the receipt of your letter of the 5th inst. (January, 1785), surprise or gratitude. Both were greater than I have words to express. The attention and good wishes, which the Assembly have evidenced by their act for vesting in me one hundred and fifty shares in the navigation of the Rivers Potomac and James, are more than mere compliment. There is an unequivocal and substantial meaning annexed. But believe me, sir, notwithstanding this, no circumstance has happened to me since I left the walks of public life, which has so much embarrassed me. On the one hand,

I consider this act, as I have already observed, as a noble and unequivocal proof of the good opinion, the affection, and disposition of my country to serve me; and I should be hurt, if, by declining the acceptance of it, my refusal should be construed into disrespect, or the smallest slight upon the generous intention of the country; or it should be thought that an ostentatious display of disinterestedness, or public virtue, was the source of refusal. On the other hand, it is really my wish to have my mind, and my actions, which are the result of reflection, as free and independent as the air; that I may be more at liberty (in things which my opportunities and experience have brought me to the knowledge of) to express my sentiments, and, if necessary, to suggest what may occur to me under the fullest conviction, that, although my judgment may be arraigned, there may be no suspicion that sinister motives had the smallest influence in the suggestion. Not content, then, with the bare consciousness of my having, in all this navigation business, acted upon the clearest conviction of the political importance of the measure, I would wish that every individual who may hear that it was a favorite plan of mine, may know, also, that I had no other motive for promoting it, than the advantage of which I conceived it would be productive to the Union, and to this State in particular, by cementing the eastern and western territory together; at the same time that it will give vigor and increase to our commerce, and be a convenience to our citizens.

How would this matter be viewed, then, by the eye of the world, and what would be the opinion of it, when it comes to be related, that George Washington has received twenty thousand dollars and five thousand pounds sterling of the public money as an interest therein! Would not this, in the estimation of it (if I am entitled to any merit for the part I have acted, and without it there is no foundation for the act), deprive me of the principal thing which is laudable in my conduct? Would it not, in some respects, be considered in the same light as a pension? And would not the apprehension of this make me more reluctantly offer my sentiments in future? In a word, under whatever pretence, and however customarily these gratuitous gifts are made in other countries, should I not thenceforward be considered as a dependent? one moment's thought of which would give me more pain than I should receive pleasure from the product of all the tolls, were every farthing of them vested in me, although I consider it as one of the most certain and increasing estates in the country.

I have written to you with an openness becoming our friendship. I could have said more on the subject, but I have already said enough to let you into the state of my mind. I wish to know whether the ideas I entertain occurred to, and were expressed by, any member in or out of the House. Upon the whole you may be assured, my dear sir, that my mind is not a little agitated. I want the best information and advice to settle it. I have no inclination, as I have already observed, to avail myself of the generosity of the country; nor do I wish to appear ostentatiously disinterested (for more than probably my refusal would be ascribed to this motive); nor that the country should harbor an idea that I am disposed to set little value on her favors, the manner of granting which is as flattering as the grant is important. My present difficulties, however, shall be no impediment to the progress of the undertaking. I will receive the full and frank opinions of my friends with thankfulness. I shall have time enough between the sitting of the next Assembly to consider the tendency of the act; and in this, as in all other matters, will endeavor to decide for the best.

EXTRACT FROM A LETTER TO RICHARD HENRY LEE, PRESIDENT OF CONGRESS.

MOUNT VERNON, February 8, 1785.

Since my last, I have had the honor to receive your favors of the 26th of December and 16th of January. I have now the pleasure to inform you that the Assemblies of Virginia and Maryland have enacted laws, of which the inclosed is a copy. They are exactly similar in both States. At the same time, and at the joint and equal expense of the two governments, the sum of six thousand six hundred and sixty-six dollars and two-thirds is voted for opening and keeping in repair a road from the highest practicable navigation of this river to that of the River Cheat, or Monongahela, as commissioners, who are appointed to survey and lay out the same, shall find most convenient and beneficial to the western settlers; and they have concurred in an application to the State of Pennsylvania for permission to open another road from Fort Cumberland to the Youghiogheny, at the Three Forks, or Turkey Foot. A similar bill to the one inclosed is passed by our Assembly respecting the navigation of James River, and the communication between it and the waters of the Great Kenawha. And the Executive has been authorized, by a resolve of the Assembly, to appoint commissioners to examine and report the most convenient course for a canal between Elizabeth River and the waters of the Roanoke, with an estimate of the expense; and if the last communication shall be found to require the concurrence of North Carolina, to make application to the legislature thereof accordingly.

EXTRACT FROM A LETTER TO DAVID HUMPHREYS.

MOUNT VERNON, July 25, 1785.

My attention is more immediately engaged in a project, which I think big with great political, as well as commercial, advantages to the States, especially the middle ones; it is by removing the obstructions and extending the inland navigation of our rivers, to bring the States on the Atlantic in close connection with those forming to the westward, by a short and easy transportation.

Without this, I can easily conceive they will have different views, separate interests, and other connections. I may be singular in my ideas, but they are these: that, to open a door to, and make easy the way for, those settlers to the westward (who ought to advance regularly and compactly) before we make any stir about the navigation of the Mississippi, and before our settlements are far advanced towards that river, would be our true line of policy. It can, I think, be demonstrated that the produce of the western territory (if the navigations which are in hand succeed, of which I have no doubt), as low down the Ohio as the Great Kenawha, and I believe to the Falls, and between the ports above the lakes, may be brought either to the highest shipping port on the Potomac or James Rivers, at a less expense, with more ease, including the return, and in a much shorter time, than it can be carried to New Orleans, if the Spaniards, instead of restrictions, were to throw open their ports and invite our trade. But if the commerce of that country should embrace this channel, and connections be formed, experience has taught us, and there is a very recent proof with Great Britain, how next to impracticable it is to divert it; and, if that should be the case, the Atlantic States, especially as those to the westward will in a great degree be filled with foreigners, will be no more to the present Union, except to excite perhaps very justly our fears, than the country of California is, which is still more to the westward, and belonging to another power.

The following extract is taken from General Washington's interesting letter to Edmund Randolph, dated Mount Vernon, July 30th, 1785, relative to his disposition of the donation from the State of Virginia. It is an additional evidence of the high value he placed upon that interest, and the importance with which he regarded the improvements to which it refers.

Although it is not my intention to derive any pecuniary advantage from the generous vote of the Assembly of this State, in consequence of its gratuitous gift of shares in the navigation of each of the Rivers Potomac and James; yet, as I consider these undertakings of vast political and commercial importance to the States of the Atlantic, especially to those nearest the centre of the Union, and adjoining the western territory, I can let no act of mine impede the progress of the work. I have therefore come to the determination to hold the shares, which the Treasurer was directed to subscribe for on my account, in trust for the use and benefit of the public; unless I should be able to discover, before the meeting of the Assembly, that it would be agreeable to it to have the product of the tolls arising from these shares applied as a fund in which to establish two charity schools, one on each river, for the education and support of the children of the poor in this country, particularly the children of those men of this description, who have fallen in the defence of the rights and liberties of it. If the plan succeeds, of which I have no doubt, I am sure it will be a very productive and increasing fund, and the moneys thus applied will be a beneficial institution.

I am aware that my non-acceptance of these shares will have various motives ascribed to it, among which an ostentatious display of disinterestedness, perhaps the charge of disrespect or slight of the favors of my country, may lead the van; but under a consciousness that my conduct herein is not influenced by considerations of this nature, and that I shall act more agreeably to my own feelings, and more consistently with my early declarations, by declining to accept them, I shall not only hope for indulgence, but a favorable interpretation of my conduct. My friends, I persuade myself, will acquit me, the world, I hope, will judge charitably.

Previous to the advertisements of Messrs. Cabell, Buchanan, and Southall, that half the sum required by the act for opening and extending the navigation of James River, is subscribed, and the 20th of next month appointed for the subscribers to meet at Richmond, I take the liberty of giving you a power to act for me on that occasion. I would (having the accomplishment of this navigation much at heart) have attended in person, but the President and Directors of the Potomac Company, by their own appointment, are to commence the survey of this river in the early part of next month; for which purpose I shall leave home to-morrow.

EXTRACT OF A LETTER TO RICHARD HENRY LEE, PRESIDENT OF CONGRESS.

MOUNT VERNON, August 22, 1785.

In my absence with the Directors of the Potomac navigation, to examine the river, and fix a plan of operations, your favor, begun on the 23d, and ended on the 31st of July, came to this place. I am sorry to hear of your late indisposition, but congratulate you on your recovery, hoping the re-establishment of your health may be of long continuance.

* * * * * * *

It is to be hoped that our minister at the Court of London will bring that government to an explanation respecting the western posts which it still retains on the American side of the line, contrary to the spirit, if not to the letter of the treaty. My opinion from the first, and so I declared it, was, that these posts would be detained from us as long as they could be held under any pretence whatsoever. I have not changed it, though I wish for cause to do so, as it may become a serious matter. However singular the opinion may be, I cannot divest myself of it, that the navigation of the Mississippi *at this time* ought to be no object with us. On the contrary, until we have a little time allowed to open and make easy the way between the Atlantic States and the western territory, the obstructions had better remain. There is nothing which binds one country or one State to another but interest. With all this cement, the western inhabitants, who more than probably will be composed in a great degree of foreigners, can have no predilection for us, and a commercial connection is the only tie we can have upon them. It is clear to me that the trade of the lakes, and of the River Ohio, as low as the Great Kenawha, if not to the Falls, may be brought to the Atlantic ports easier and cheaper, taking the whole voyage together, than it can be carried to New Orleans; but, once open the door to the latter before the obstructions are removed from the former, let commercial connections, which lead to others, be formed, and the habit of that trade be well established, and it will be found to be no easy matter to divert it; and *vice versa*. When the settlements are stronger and more extended to the westward, the navigation of the Mississippi will be an object of importance, and we shall then be able to speak a more efficacious language, than policy, I think, dictates at present.

EXTRACT FROM A LETTER TO WILLIAM GRAYSON, MEMBER OF CONGRESS.

MOUNT VERNON, August 22, 1785.

During my tour up the Potomac River, with the Directors, to examine and to form a plan for opening and extending the navigation of it, agreeably to the Acts of Virginia and Maryland Assemblies, your favor of the 25th came to this place.

* * * * * * *

We have got the Potomac navigation in hand. Workmen are

employed, under the best manager and assistants we could obtain, at the Falls of Shenandoah and Seneca; and I am happy to inform you, that upon a critical examination of them by the directors, the manager, and myself, we are unanimously of opinion that the difficulties at these two places do not exceed the expectations we had formed of them; and that the navigation through them might be effected without the aid of locks. How far we may have been deceived with respect to the first, as the water, though low, may yet fall, I shall not decide; but we are not mistaken, I think, in our conjecture of the other.

EXTRACT FROM A LETTER TO ARTHUR ST. CLAIR.

Mount Vernon, August 31, 1785.

Your favor of the 21st ult., inclosing a letter written in behalf of the Society of the Cincinnati, in the State of Pennsylvania, on the 9th of July, in the preceding year, came to this place in my absence on a tour up the River Potomac.

EXTRACT FROM A LETTER TO THOMAS JEFFERSON.

Mount Vernon, September 26, 1785.

I am very happy to find that your sentiments respecting the interest the Assembly was pleased to give me in the navigation of the Potomac and James Rivers, coincide with my own. I never for a moment entertained an idea of accepting it. The difficulty with which my mind labored was how to refuse without giving offence. Ultimately I have it in contemplation to apply the profits arising from the tolls to some public use. In this, if I knew how, I would meet the wishes of the Assembly; but if I am not able to come at these, my own inclination leads me to apply them to the establishment of two charity schools, one on each river, for the education and support of poor children, especially the descendants of those who have fallen in defence of their country.

EXTRACT FROM A LETTER TO PATRICK HENRY, GOVERNOR OF VIRGINIA.

MOUNT VERNON, October, 29, 1785.

Your excellency having been pleased to transmit to me a copy of the act appropriating for my benefit certain shares in the companies for opening the navigation of James and Potomac Rivers, I take the liberty of returning to the General Assembly, through your hands, the profound and grateful acknowledgments inspired by so signal a mark of their beneficent intentions towards me. I beg you, sir, to assure them, that I am filled on this occasion, with every sentiment which can flow from a heart warm with love for my country, sensible to every token of its approbation and affection, and solicitous to testify in every instance a respectful submission to its wishes.

With these sentiments in my bosom, I need not dwell on the anxiety I feel in being obliged, in this instance, to decline a favor which is rendered no less flattering by the manner in which it is conveyed, than it is affectionate in itself. In explaining this observation, I pass over a comparison of my endeavors in the public service, with the many honorable testimonials of approbation which have already so far overrated and overpaid them, reciting one consideration only, which supersedes the necessity of recurring to any other.

When I was first called to the station with which I was honored during the late conflict for our liberties, to the diffidence which I had so many reasons to feel in accepting it, I thought it my duty to join a firm resolution to shut my hand against every pecuniary recompense. To this resolution I have invariably adhered, and from it, if I had the inclination, I do not feel at liberty now to depart.

Whilst I repeat, therefore, my fervent acknowledgments to the legislature, for their very kind sentiments and intentions in my favor, and at the same time beg them to be persuaded that a remembrance of this singular proof of their goodness towards me will never cease to cherish returns of the warmest affection and gratitude, I must pray that their act, so far as it has for its object my personal emolument, may not have its effect. But if it should please the General Assembly to permit me to turn the destination of the fund vested in me, from my private emolument, to objects of a public nature, it will be my study in selecting these, to prove the sincerity of my gratitude for the honor conferred on me, by proposing such as may appear most subservient to the enlightened and patriotic views of the legislature.

EXTRACT FROM A LETTER TO HENRY LEE, IN CONGRESS.

MOUNT VERNON, June 18, 1786.

The advantages with which the inland navigation of the Rivers Potomac and James, are pregnant, must strike every mind that reasons upon the subject; but there is, I perceive, a diversity of sentiment respecting the benefits and the consequences which may flow from the free and immediate use of the Mississippi. My opinion of this matter has been uniformly the same, and no light in which I have been able to consider the subject is likely to change it. It is, neither to relinquish nor to push our claims to this navigation, but in the meanwhile to open *all* the communications which nature has afforded, between the Atlantic States and the western territory, and to encourage the use of them to the utmost. In my judgment, it is a matter of very serious concern to the well-being of the former, to make it the interest of the latter to trade with them; without which the ties of consanguinity, which are weakening every day, will soon be no bond, and we shall be no more, a few years hence, to the inhabitants of that country, than the British and Spaniards are at this day; not so much, indeed, because commercial connections, it is well known, lead to others, and united are difficult to be broken. These must take place with the Spaniards, if the navigation of the Mississippi is opened.

Clear I am that it would be for the interest of the western settlers as low down the Ohio as the Big Kenawha, and back to the lakes, to bring their produce through one of the channels I have named; but the way must be cleared, and made easy and obvious to them, or else the ease with which people glide down the streams will give a different bias to their thinking and acting. Whenever the new States become so populous and so extended to the westward as really to need it, there will be no power which can deprive them of the use of the Mississippi. Why, then, should we prematurely urge a matter which is displeasing, and may produce disagreeable consequences, if it is our interest to let it sleep? It may require some management to quiet the restless and impetuous spirits of Kentucky, of whose conduct I am more apprehensive in this business, than I am of all the opposition that will be given by the Spaniards.

EXTRACT FROM A LETTER TO THOMAS JEFFERSON.

MOUNT VERNON, August 1, 1786.

We have no news of importance; and, if we had, I should hardly be in the way of learning it, as I divide my time between the superintendence of opening the navigation of our rivers, and attention to my private concerns.

EXTRACT FROM A LETTER TO BUSHROD WASHINGTON.

MOUNT VERNON, September 30, 1786.

I was from home when your servant arrived, and found him in a hurry to be gone when I returned! I have company in the house, and am on the eve of a journey up the river to meet the Directors of the Potomac Company. These things continuing will not allow me time to give any explicit answer to the question you have propounded.

EXTRACT FROM A LETTER TO RICHARD BUTLER, SUPERINTENDENT OF INDIAN AFFAIRS.

MOUNT VERNON, November 27, 1786.

Your appointment gave me pleasure, as everything will do, which contributes to your satisfaction and emolument, because I have a sincere regard for you. In your leisure hours, whilst you remain on the Ohio in discharge of the trust reposed in you, I should be glad to know the real temper and designs of the western Indians, and the situation of affairs in that country. As I am anxious to learn the nature of the navigation of Beaver Creek, the distance, and what kind of portage there is between it and Cayahoga, or any other nearer navigable water of Lake Erie, and the nature of the navigation of the latter; and also the navigation of the Muskingum, the distance and sort of portage across to the navigable waters of Cayahoga or Sandusky, and the kind of navigation therein; you would do me an acceptable favor to convey them to me, with the computed distances from the River Ohio by each of these routes to the lake itself.

EXTRACT FROM A LETTER TO RICHARD HENRY LEE.

PHILADELPHIA, July 19, 1787.

I have had the honor to receive your favor of the 15th inst., and thank you for the ordinance which was inclosed in it. My sentiments, with respect to the navigation of the Mississippi have been long fixed, and are not dissimilar to those which are expressed in your letter. I have ever been of opinion, that the true policy of the Atlantic States, instead of contending prematurely for the free navigation of that river (which eventually, and perhaps as soon as it will be our true interest to obtain it, must happen), would be to open and improve the natural communications with the western country, through which the produce of it might be transported with convenience and ease to our markets. Till you get low down the Ohio, I conceive, that, considering the length of the voyage to New Orleans, the difficulty of the current, and the time necessary to perform it in, it would be the interest of the inhabitants to bring their produce to our ports; and sure I am there is no other tie by which they will long form a link in the chain of federal union. I believe, however, from the temper in which these people appear to be, and from the ambitious and turbulent spirit of some of their demagogues, that it has become a moot-point to determine, when every circumstance which attends this business is brought into view, what is best to be done. The State of Virginia having taken the matter up with so high a hand, is not among the least embarrassing or disagreeable parts of the difficulty.

EXTRACT FROM GENERAL WASHINGTON'S LETTER TO THOMAS JEFFERSON.

MOUNT VERNON, January 1, 1788.

I have received your favor of the 14th of August, and am sorry that it is not in my power to give any further information relative to the practicability of opening a communication between Lake Erie and the Ohio, than you are already possessed of. I have made frequent inquiries since the time of your writing at Annapolis, but could never collect anything that was decided or satisfactory. I have again renewed them, and flatter myself with better prospects.

The accounts generally agree as to its being a flat country between the waters of Lake Erie and the Big Beaver, but differ very much with respect to the distance between their sources, their navigation, and the inconveniences which would attend the cutting of a canal between them. From the best information I have been able to obtain of that country, the sources of the Muskingum and Cayahoga approach nearer to each other than the Big Beaver; but a communication through the Muskingum would be more circuitous and difficult, having the Ohio to a greater extent to ascend, unless the latter could be avoided by opening a communication between James River and the Great Kenawha, or between the Little Kenawha and the west branch of the Monongahela, which is said to be very practicable by a short portage. As a proof of this, a road is now opened, or opening, under the authority, and at the expense of the States of Virginia and Maryland, from the north branch of the Potomac, commencing at the mouth of Savage River to Cheat River; and continued from thence to the navigable waters of the Little Kenawha at the cost of the former.

The distance between Lake Erie and the Ohio through the Big

Beaver, is, however, so much less than the route through the Muskingum, that it would, in my opinion, operate very strongly in favor of opening a canal between the sources of the nearest water of the Lake and the Big Beaver, although the distance between them should be much greater, and the operation more difficult than to the Muskingum, as it is the direct line to the nearest shipping port in the Atlantic. I shall omit no opportunity of gaining every information relative to this important subject, and with pleasure communicate to you whatever may be worthy of your attention.

EXTRACT FROM A LETTER TO RICHARD BUTLER.

MOUNT VERNON, January 10, 1788.

As you have had opportunities of gaining extensive knowledge and information respecting the western territory, its situation, rivers, and the face of the country, I must beg the favor of you, my dear sir, to resolve the following queries, either from your own knowledge, or certain information, as well to gratify my own curiosity as to enable me to satisfy several gentlemen of distinction in other countries, who have applied to me for information upon the subject.

1. What is the face of the country between the sources, or canoe navigation of the Cayahoga, which empties itself into Lake Erie and the Big Beaver, and between the Cayahoga and the Muskingum ?

2. The distance between the waters of the Cayahoga and each of the two rivers above mentioned ?

3. Would it be practicable, and not very expensive, to cut a canal between the Cayahoga and either of the above rivers, so as to open a communication between the waters of Lake Erie and the Ohio ?

4. Whether there is any more direct, practicable, and easy communication, than these between the waters of Lake Erie and those of the Ohio, by which the fur and peltry of the upper country can be transported ?

Any information you can give me, relative to the above queries, from your own knowledge, will be most agreeable, but if that is not sufficiently accurate for you to decide upon, the best and most authentic accounts of others will be very acceptable.

EXTRACT FROM A LETTER TO WILLIAM IRVINE.

MOUNT VERNON, February 18, 1788.

I have to acknowledge the receipt of your favor of the 27th ult., and to thank you for the information contained in it. As a communication between the waters of Lake Erie and those of the Ohio is a matter which promises great public utility, and as every step towards the investigation of it may be considered as promoting the general interest of our country, I need make no apology to you for any trouble that I have given upon this subject.

I am fully sensible that no account can be sufficiently accurate to hazard any operations upon, without an actual survey. My object in wishing a solution of the queries proposed to you, was that I might be enabled to return answers, in some degree satisfactory, to several gentlemen of distinction in foreign countries, who have applied to me for information on the subject, in behalf of others who wish to engage in the fur trade, and, at the same time, to gratify my own curiosity, and assist me in forming a judgment of the practicability of opening a communication, should it ever be seriously in contemplation.

1. Could a channel once be opened to convey the fur and peltry from the lakes into the eastern country, its advantages would be so obvious as to induce an opinion that it would, in a short time,

become the channel of conveyance for much the greater part of the commodities brought from thence.

2. The trade, which has been carried on between New York and that quarter, is subject to great inconveniences from the length of the communication, number of portages, and at seasons from ice, yet it has, notwithstanding, been prosecuted with success.

I shall feel myself much obliged, by any further information that you may find time and inclination to communicate to me on this head.

EXTRACT FROM A LETTER TO RICHARD HENDERSON.

MOUNT VERNON, June 19, 1788.

In the first place, it is a point conceded, that America, under an efficient government, will be the most favorable country of any in the world for persons of industry and frugality, possessed of a moderate capital. It is also believed, that it will not be less advantageous to the happiness of the lowest class of people, on account of the equal distribution of property, the great plenty of unoccupied lands, and the facility of procuring the means of subsistence. The scheme of purchasing a good tract of freehold estate, and bringing out a number of able-bodied men, indented for a certain time, appears to be indisputably a national one.

All the interior arrangements of transferring the property, and commencing the establishment, you are as well acquainted with as I can possibly be. It might be considered a point of more difficulty to decide upon the place which should be most proper for a settlement. Although I believe that emigrants from other countries to this, who shall be well disposed, and conduct themselves properly, would be treated with equal friendship and kindness in *all* parts of it; yet, in the old-settled States, land is so much occupied, and the value so much enhanced by the contiguous cultivation, that the price would, in general, be an objection. The land in the western country, or that on the Ohio, like all others, has its advantages and disadvantages. The neighborhood of the savages, and the difficulty of transportation, are the great objections. The danger of the first will soon cease by the strong establishments now taking place; the inconveniences of the second will be in a great degree remedied, by opening the internal navigation. No colony in America was ever settled under such favorable auspices as that which has just commenced at the Muskingum. Information, property, and strength will be its characteristics. I know many of the settlers personally, and there never were men better calculated to promote the welfare of such a community.

If I was a young man, just preparing to begin the world, or if advanced in life, and had a family to make a provision for, I know of no country where I should rather fix my habitation than in some part of that region for which the writer of the queries seems to have a predilection. He might be informed that his namesake and distant relation, General St. Clair, is not only in high repute, but that he is Governor of all the territory westward of the Ohio, and that there is a gentleman (Mr. Joel Barlow) gone from New York by the last French packet, who will be in London in the course of this year, and, also, is authorized to dispose of a very large body of land in that country.

EXTRACT FROM A LETTER TO THOMAS JEFFERSON.

MOUNT VERNON, August 31, 1788.

I was very much gratified a little time ago by the receipt of your letter dated the 2d of May. You have my best thanks for the political information contained in it, as well as for the satisfactory account of the canal of Languedoc. It gives me great pleasure to be made acquainted with the particulars of that stupendous work, though I do not expect to derive any but speculative advantages from it.

When America will be able to embark in projects of such pecuniary extent, I know not; probably not for very many years to come; but it will be a good example, and not without its use, if we can carry our present undertakings happily into effect. Of this we have now the fairest prospect. Notwithstanding the real scarcity of money, and the difficulty of collecting it, the laborers employed by the Potomac Company have made very great progress in removing the obstructions at the Shenandoah, Seneca, and Great Falls; insomuch that, if this summer had not proved unusually rainy, and if we could have had a favorable autumn, the navigation might have been sufficiently opened (though not completed) for boats to pass from Fort Cumberland to within nine miles of a shipping port, by the first of January next. There remains now no doubt of the practicability of the plan, or that, upon the ulterior operations being performed, they will become the great avenue into the western country; a country which is now settling in an extraordinarily rapid manner, under uncommonly favorable circumstances, and which promises to afford a capacious asylum for the poor and persecuted of the earth.

EXTRACT FROM A LETTER TO WILLIAM IRVINE.

MOUNT VERNON, October 31, 1788.

The letter with which you favored me, dated the 6th instant, inclosing a sketch of the waters near the line which separates your State from that of New York, came duly to hand, for which I offer you my acknowledgments and thanks.

The extensive inland navigation with which this country abounds, and the easy communications which many of the rivers afford with the amazing territory to the westward of us, will certainly be productive of infinite advantage to the Atlantic States, if the legislatures of those through which they pass have liberality and public spirit enough to improve them. For my part, I wish sincerely that every door to that country may be set wide open, that the commercial intercourse with it may be rendered as free and as easy as possible. This, in my judgment, is the best, if not the only cement that can bind those people to us for any length of time; and we shall, I think, be deficient in forethought and wisdom if we neglect the means to effect it. Our interest is so much in unison with the policy of the measure, that nothing but that ill-timed and misapplied parsimony, and contracted way of thinking which intermingles so much in all our public councils, can counteract it.

If the Chatauque Lake, at the head of Conewango River, approximates Lake Erie as nearly as is laid down in the draft you sent me, it presents a very short portage indeed between the two, and an access to all those above the latter.

EXTRACT FROM A LETTER TO WILLIAM GORDON.

MOUNT VERNON, December 23, 1788.

This much I thought it might be well to say, in apology for my not being able to comply with your request. Indeed, when you consider the domestic walks of life in which I pass my days, the multiplicity of private concerns in which I am involved, the numerous epistolary applications from different quarters, the round of company I have at my house, and the avocations occasioned by my being at the head of the company for clearing the Potomac, you will do me the justice to suppose that I can have few topics or little time for correspondences of mere friendship, ceremony, or speculation.

EXTRACT FROM A LETTER TO THOMAS JEFFERSON.

MOUNT VERNON, February 13, 1789.

A desire of encouraging whatever is useful and economical seems now generally to prevail. Several capital artists in different branches have lately arrived in the country. A factory of glass is established upon a large scale on Monocacy River, near Frederick-town, in Maryland. I am informed it will this year produce glass of various kinds nearly to the amount of ten thousand pounds value. This factory will be essentially benefited by having the navigation of the Potomac completely opened. But the total benefits of that navigation will not be confined to narrower limits than the extent of the whole western territory of the United States.

You have been made acquainted, my dear sir, with my ideas of the practicability, importance and extent of that navigation, as they have been occasionally, though fully expressed, in my several letters to you. Notwithstanding my constant and utmost endeavors to obtain precise information respecting the nearest and best communication between the Ohio and Lake Erie, I am not yet able to add anything more satisfactory to the observations which I have had the honor to make on that subject; but I have lately received a correct draft executed principally from actual surveys of the country between the sources of the Potomac and those navigable waters that fall into the Ohio. Of this I inclose you such a rough sketch as my avocations would permit me to make; my principal object being to show, that the distance between the two waters is shorter, and that the means of communication are easier than I had hitherto represented or imagined. I need not describe what and how extensive the rivers are, which will be thus in a wonderful manner connected as soon as the Potomac shall be rendered entirely passable. The passage would have been opened from Fort Cumberland to the Great Falls (nine miles from tide-water) before this time, as I mentioned in my letter of the 31st of August last, had it not been for the unfavorableness of the season. In spite of that untoward circumstance, I have the pleasure to inform you, that two or three boats have actually arrived at the last-mentioned place.

I am going on Monday next to visit the works as far as the Seneca Falls. Could I have delayed writing the letter until my return from thence, and afterwards availed myself of the same conveyance, I might have been more particular in my account of the state of the several works, and especially of the situation of the land adjoining the canal at the Great Falls. Whensoever the produce of the parts of the country bordering on the sources of the Potomac, and contiguous to the long rivers that run into it (particularly the Shenandoah and South Branch), shall be water-borne down to tide-water for exportation, I conceive this place must become very valuable. From the conveniency of the basin a little above the spot where the locks are to be placed, and from the inducements which will be superadded by several fine mill-seats, I cannot entertain a doubt of the establishment of a town in that place. Indeed, mercantile people are desirous that the event should take place as soon as possible. Manufactures of various commodities, and in iron particularly, will doubtless be carried on to advantage there. The mill-seats I know have long been considered as very valuable ones. How far buildings erected upon them may be exposed to injuries from freshets or the breaking up of the ice, I am not competent to determine from my own knowledge; but the opinion of persons better acquainted with these matters than I am, is, that they may be rendered secure. On the commodiousness of Alexandria for carrying on the fur trade throughout the whole western country, I treated in a very minute, and I may say, almost voluminous manner, in my communication to you on the 30th of May, 1787. Probably Georgetown and the place which I have just mentioned, will participate largely and happily in the great emoluments to be derived from that and other valuable articles, through the inland navigation of the upper and western country.

EXTRACT FROM A LETTER TO HARRY INNES.

MOUNT VERNON, March 2, 1789.

I have been favored by the receipt of your obliging letter, dated the 18th of December last, just in time to send my acknowledgments by a person who is immediately returning to Kentucky. This circumstance prevents me from expressing so fully as I might otherwise have done, the sense I have of the very patriotic sentiments you entertain respecting the important matter which is the subject of your letter. As a friend to United America, I embrace with extreme satisfaction the proposals you are pleased to offer of transmitting further intelligence. For which purpose I will endeavor to arrange and send you a cipher by the earliest safe conveyance. In the mean time, I rely implicitly upon that honor which you have pledged, and those professions which you have made; and sincerely hope, that your activity and discretion will be successful in developing.

The following extracts of a correspondence between the Earl of Buchan, a Scotch nobleman, eminent for his learning, his Christian virtues, and the benevolence of his heart, and General Washington, form an appropriate and graceful conclusion to the *Third Part* of this compilation.

DRYBURG ABBEY, June 28, 1791.

SIR: I had the honor to receive your Excellency's letter, relating to the advertisement of Dr. Anderson's periodical publication, in the Gazette of the United States; which attention to my recommendation, I feel very sensibly, and return you my grateful acknowledgments.

In the 21st No. of that Literary Miscellany, I inserted a monetary paper, respecting America, which I flatter myself may, if attended to on the other side of the Atlantic, be productive of good consequences.

To use your own emphatic words, "May that Almighty Being who rules over the universe, who presides in the councils of nations, and whose providential aid can supply every human defect, consecrate, to the liberties and happiness of the American people, a government instituted by themselves, for public and private security, upon the basis of law and equal administration of justice, preserving to every individual as much civil and political freedom as is consistent with the safety of the nation." And may *He* be pleased to continue your life and strength, as long as you can be in any way useful to your country.

Yours, &c,

BUCHAN.

PHILADELPHIA, April 22, 1793.

MY LORD: The favorable wishes which your Lordship has expressed for the prosperity of this young and rising country, cannot but be gratefully received by all its citizens and every lover of it; one mean to the contribution of which, and its happiness, is very judiciously portrayed in the following words of your letter: "To be little heard of in the great world of politics."

These words, I can assure your Lordship, are an expression of my sentiments on this head; and I believe it is the sincere wish of United America to have nothing to do with the political intrigues or squabbles of European nations; but, on the contrary, to exchange commodities, and live in peace and amity with all the inhabitants of the earth; and this, I am persuaded, they will do, if rightfully it can be done.

To administer justice to, and receive it from every power they are connected with, will, I hope, be always found the most prominent feature in the administration of this country; and, I flatter myself, that nothing short of imperious necessity can occasion a breach with any of them. Under such a system, if we are allowed to pursue it, the agriculture and mechanical arts—the wealth and population of these States, will increase with that degree of rapidity, as to baffle all calculations, and must surpass any idea your Lordship can hitherto have entertained on the occasion.

I am, &c.,

G. WASHINGTON.

TO THE EARL OF BUCHAN, &c. &c.

THE END.

APPENDIX.

APPENDIX.

A.

To George Washington, Esquire, one of the Adjutants General of the Troops and Forces in the Colony of Virginia.

I, reposing especial trust and confidence in the ability, conduct, and fidelity of you, the said George Washington, have appointed you my express messenger; and you are hereby authorized and empowered to proceed hence with all convenient and possible dispatch, to that place on the River Ohio, where the French have lately erected a fort or forts, or where the commandant of the French forces resides, in order to deliver my letter and message to him, and after waiting not exceeding one week for an answer, you are to take your leave and return immediately back.

To this communication, I have set my hand and caused the great seal of this dominion to be affixed, at the city of Williamsburg, the seat of my government, this 30th day of October, in the twenty-seventh year of the reign of his Majesty George the Second, King of Great Britain, &c. &c.

ROBERT DINWIDDIE.

Annoque Domini, 1753.

B.

Instructions for George Washington.

Whereas, I have received information of a body of French forces being assembled in a hostile manner on the River Ohio, intending by force of arms to erect certain forts on the said river within this territory, and contrary to the dignity and peace of our sovereign and King of Great Britain:

These are, therefore, to require and direct you, the said George Washington, forthwith to repair to Logstown, on the said River Ohio, and having there informed yourself where the said French forces have posted themselves, thereupon to proceed to such place; and being there arrived, to present your credentials, together with my letter, to the chief commanding officer, and in the name of his Britannic Majesty to demand an answer thereto.

On your arrival at Logstown, you are to address yourself to the half king, to Monacotoicha, and other the sachems of the Six Nations, acquainting them with your orders to visit and deliver my letter to the French commanding officer, and desiring the said chiefs to appoint you a sufficient number of their warriors to be your safeguard, as near the French as you may desire, and to wait your further directions.

You are diligently to inquire into the number and force of the French on the Ohio, and the adjacent country; how they are likely to be assisted from Canada; and what are the difficulties and conveniences of that communication, and the time required for it.

You are to take care to be truly informed what forts the

French have erected, and where; how they are garrisoned and appointed, and what is their distance from each other, and from Logstown; and from the best intelligence you can procure, your are to learn what gave occasion to this expedition of the French; how they are likely to be supported, and what their pretensions are.

When the French commandant has given you the required and necessary dispatches, you are to desire of him a proper guard to protect you as far on your return as you may judge for your safety, against any straggling Indians or hunters that may be ignorant of your character, and molest you.

Wishing you good success in your negotiation, and a safe and speedy return,

I am, &c.,

ROBERT DINWIDDIE.

WILLIAMSBURG, October 30, 1753.

C.

TO ALL TO WHOM THESE PRESENTS MAY COME OR CONCERN, GREETING:

Whereas, I have appointed George Washington, Esquire, by commission, under the great seal, my express messenger to the commandant of the French forces on the River Ohio, and as he is charged with business of great importance to his majesty, and this Dominion:

I do hereby command all his majesty's subjects, and particularly require all in alliance and amity with the crown of

Great Britain, and all others to whom this *passport* may come agreeably to the law of nations, to be aiding and assisting, as a safeguard to the said George Washington, and his attendants, in his present passage to and from the River Ohio, as aforesaid.

ROBERT DINWIDDIE.

D.

Fort Cumberland was constructed on the west bank of Wills' Creek, near its junction with the Potomac River. It was a breastwork of earth, of irregular form. The name was given to it by general Braddock in honor of the Duke of Cumberland, through whose influence with the court he was selected to take command of the troops.

The Duke was an accomplished officer; had served with great distinction in Flanders, and was an universal favorite with the army. When the civil commotions took place between England and Scotland, this distinguished nobleman was appointed to the command of the King's forces in Edinburgh, amounting to about 14,000 men.

E.

The "*Great Meadows*" is a piece of flat land situated in the valley of a small stream which empties into the Youghiogheny River on the west side of Laurel Hill, and about 500 yards south of the national road.

The battle was fought on the 3d day of July, 1754.

It was the intention of Col. Washington, and the decision of the council of war, which was held while he occupied with his small force an encampment on the southwest side of the hill, that as soon as it was ascertained that the French and their Indian allies had determined to march against them, to retire from that position to Gist's plantation on the northeast side of the hill, and entrench himself there, and make a stand against the enemy. But time did not allow this plan to be carried into effect. The scouting and spying parties returned and reported that the enemy in combined force were on their march to make an attack. The men under the command of Colonel Washington were much fatigued from incessant toil for some time; they were also short of provisions. He determined, therefore, to halt his command at the first advantageous position he could reach with the swivels and baggage, and the few horses he had with him. This spot, so memorable in history, was the *Great Meadows.* Here he hastily threw up an entrenchment, and at eleven o'clock in the forenoon of the same day, the enemy appeared, and with the usual yells of the savages, the enemy rushed upon the entrenched camp; but were met and repelled with the loss of several hundred French and their Indian allies.

F.

Colonel George Washington was appointed Commander-in-Chief of the American army, by the unanimous vote of the first Congress, which convened in Philadelphia, on the 15th day of June, 1775, and of which he was a member.

The following proceedings on that occasion, are copied from the Journal.

IN CONGRESS, *Thursday*, June 15, 1775.

Resolved, That a General be appointed to command all the continental forces raised, or to be raised, for the defence of American liberty.

That five hundred dollars per month be allowed for the pay and expenses of the General.

The Congress then proceeded to the choice of a General, by ballot, and George Washington, Esq., was unanimously elected.

Friday, June 16, 1775.

The President informed Colonel Washington that the Congress had, yesterday, unanimously made choice of him to be General and Commander-in-Chief of the American forces, and requested he would accept of that employment; to which Colonel Washington, standing in his place, as a member of the House, answered:—

Mr. PRESIDENT:

Though I am truly sensible of the high honor done me in this appointment, yet I feel great distress from a consciousness that my abilities and military experience may not be equal to the extensive and important trust; however, as the Congress desire it, I will enter upon the momentous duty, and exert every power I possess in their service, for the support of the glorious cause. I beg they will accept my most cordial thanks for this distinguished testimony of their approbation.

But lest some event should happen unfavorable to my reputation, I beg it may be remembered by every gentleman in the room, that I this day declare, with the utmost sincerity, I do not think myself equal to the command I am honored with.

With respect to pay, sir, I must beg leave to assure Congress that, as no pecuniary consideration could have tempted me to accept this arduous employment, at the expense of my domestic ease and happiness, I do not wish to make any profit from it. I will keep an exact account of my expenses. These I doubt not they will discharge, and that is all I desire.

G.

December 23, 1783.

Mr. PRESIDENT:

The events on which my resignation depended having at length taken place, I have now the honor of offering my sincere congratulations to Congress, and of presenting myself before them to surrender into their hands the trust committed to me, and to claim the indulgence of retiring from the service of my country.

Happy in the confirmation of our independence and sovereignty, and pleased with the opportunity afforded the United States of becoming a respectable nation, I resign with satisfaction the appointment I accepted with diffidence, a diffidence in my abilities to accomplish so arduous a task; which, however, was superseded by a confidence in the rectitude of our cause, the support of the supreme power of the Union, and the patronage of heaven.

The successful termination of the war has verified the most sanguine expectations; and my gratitude for the interposition of Providence, and the assistance I have received from my countrymen, increases with every review of the momentous contest.

While I repeat my obligations to the army in general, I should do injustice to my own feelings not to acknowledge, in this place, the peculiar services and distinguished merits of the gentlemen who have been attached to my person during the war. It was impossible the choice of confidential officers to compose my family should have been more fortunate. Permit me, sir, to recommend in particular, those who have continued in the service to the present moment, as worthy of the favorable notice and patronage of Congress.

I consider it an indispensable duty to close this last act of my official life, by commending the interests of our dearest country to the protection of Almighty God, and those who have the superintendence of them to his holy keeping.

Having now finished the work assigned me, I retire from the theatre of action, and bidding an affectionate farewell to this august body, under whose orders I have so long acted, I here offer my commission, and take my leave of all the employments of public life.

H.

The following highly interesting letter was received from the Hon. Andrew Stewart, of Pennsylvania, in reply to an application of the compiler for information relative to an original MS. of General Washington, understood to be in his hands, indicating a route to communicate with the west nearly identical with that now proposed for the Connellsville Rail Road. The distinguished position Mr. Stewart occupied as a member of Congress, and his warm and zealous advocacy of measures of internal improvement, and his patriotic devotion to the best interests of his country, manifested both in his public and private life, the compiler regards as a sufficient apology for the liberty he has taken to introduce his letter.

UNIONTOWN, PA., March 23, 1853.

MY DEAR SIR:

Your letter of the 26th inst. is just received, and I hasten to comply with your request to furnish you with an abstract from, or reference to the original manuscript documents of General Washington, referred to in some remarks I recently made before the councils of Alleghany City, in reference to the Connellsville Road.

You will find the whole of these documents, with many

others connected with the early history of the Potomac Company (never before published), in the body and appendix to a report of 122 pages, I made from the Committee on "Roads and Canals" in Congress on the 22d of May, 1826 (27 years ago), numbered 228, and bound in Reports of Committees, House of Reps. Congress U. S., 1st Session, 19th Congress, subject, "*The Chesapeake and Ohio Canal.*" From these documents you will discover the interesting fact that as early as 1754, 20 years before the Revolution, General Washington in person explored the proposed route for connecting the east and west by the waters of the Potomac and Youghiogheny Rivers, and made a report to the Colonial Legislature of Virginia, describing all the obstructions to be overcome from Cumberland at the mouth of Wills' Creek to Georgetown, or Washington City. On the 20th of July, 1770, he made another report to the Governor of Maryland, comprehending the whole route from the Atlantic to the Ohio River at Pittsburg, by the Connellsville route, contrasting it with the Susquehanna and other connections, showing its superiority as to distance and facility of construction, and its vast importance, "as a means," to use his own words, "of becoming the channel of conveyance of the *extensive and valuable trade of a rising empire.*" If such were the views of Washington in 1770, of the importance of this route, what should be said of it now? Ought not this favorite work of the FATHER OF HIS COUNTRY to be now consummated? He finally succeeded in obtaining an act of the Virginia Legislature to incorporate a company to make this improvement.

In 1784 he went to Annapolis, in company with Gen. Lafayette, and obtained a concurrent act of the Maryland Legislature—and in a long letter, dated, "Mount Vernon, 3d Dec., 1784," addressed to James Madison and Mr. Jones, then members of the Virginia Legislature, he reiterates his views as to the great importance of opening the communication, as the best, if not the only means of keeping the eastern and western countries together, and pressing upon them the necessity of a united application by Virginia and Maryland to the Legislature of Pennsylvania, to co-operate in the construction of this work, so far as it passed through her territory, between Cumberland and Pittsburg. He also suggests the arguments to be urged, and the benefits to result to the people of Pennsylvania and the whole west for this work. Here is also displayed in a remarkable manner the wonderful sagacity of this wonderful man.

From these documents, you will further discover that as soon as General Washington was relieved from the command of the army in 1783, and before Indian hostilities had ceased, he immediately returned to this favorite plan of uniting the East and West, and filled with the idea of its importance, he mounted his horse, and at the hazard of his life actually explored in person all the present routes for connecting the Eastern and Western States (the New York, Pennsylvania, Maryland, and Virginia), and after his return in 1784, in a letter to the Marquis of Chastelleux, he says: "I have lately made a tour through the Lakes George and Champlain as far as Crown Point, then returning to Schenectady, I proceeded up the Mohawk River to Fort Schuyler, crossed over the Wood Creek, which empties into the Oneida Lake, and affords the water communication with Ontario. I then traversed the country to the head of the eastern branch of the Susquehanna, and viewed the lake Otsego, and the portage between that lake and the Mohawk River at Canajoharie. Prompted by these actual observations, I could not help taking a more contemplative and extensive view of the vast inland navigation of the United States, and could not but be struck with the immense diffusion and importance of it and with the goodness of that Providence which has dealt his favors with so profuse a hand. Would to God we may have wisdom enough to improve them! I shall not rest contented until I have explored the western country, and traversed those lines (or great part of them) which have given bounds to a new empire."

Among all the evidences of General Washington's love of country, I consider this one of the most striking. That at that early day, without fee or reward, he should have hazarded his life amid hostile Indians, and his health, sleeping in the open woods in countries then totally uninhabited, is an act of patriotic self-devotion, which we at this day can scarcely believe possible.

Among the manuscript reports of General Washington on this subject, I also found the following comparison of the several routes explored by him:—

DISTANCE FROM DETROIT TO THE SEVERAL SEAPORTS.

From Detroit, by the route through Fort Pitt and Fort Cumberland:—

	MILES.
To Alexandria (or Washington City)	607
" Richmond	840
" Philadelphia	745
" Albany	943
" New York	1103

I also found among his papers a map, made out by Gen. Washington himself, indicating the route for what he calls a "portage" between the waters of the Potomac and Youghiogheny, on the very ground, with slight variations, on which the national road was afterwards constructed. For the means of making this road, he applied to the Virginia and Maryland Legislatures—the Western people being then able, he said, to furnish little or no aid. In making these locations and maps, it appears he employed surveyors and hands, whom he paid from his own pocket. Among them I find the names of Samuel Hanaway and Dr. James Craig, the latter of whom acknowledges the receipt of £12 *7s.* and *6d.*, being his part of the expense, and who says, in one of his letters, "a general account of the expenses must be deferred until I have the pleasure of seeing you." These gentlemen made detailed reports of their operations to General Washington, which you will find in the appendix to my report, to which I refer you for these and other details equally interesting, of which you can avail yourself, if you please, in the interesting work you are about issuing. You can find them nowhere else. The original manuscript I returned to General Mason, father of the present Senator from Virginia.

Yours, very respectfully,

A. STEWART.

Col. JNO. PICKELL.

I.

One of the most important results of the policy of *internal improvement*, was the construction of the *National* or *Cumberland Road*, and to which the rapid growth of the West, in population and commercial prosperity, is mainly attributable. The compiler well recollects, as late as 1835, when that *great avenue* leading from Cumberland to the Ohio River was literally covered with horsemen, wagons, and other vehicles, forming an unbroken line, wending their way over its smooth, but hilly and mountainous surface, to the far West. Thousands of emigrants, almost daily, were seen travelling to their future homes beyond the mountains, where they planted themselves on the broad plains, in the fertile valleys, and along the borders of the numerous streams of that then distant land. By their untiring energy, toil, and perseverance, an empire of wealth and strength was added to the Union—an empire which cannot be contemplated without awakening the most patriotic feelings, and the deepest gratitude of our hearts to an overruling Providence, for the blessings vouchsafed to us as a nation—*a united family of sister States.*

K.

To the Honorable the General Assemblies
of Virginia and Maryland.

The humble petition of the President and Directors of the Potomac Company, in behalf of the said Company, showeth:

That in and by the acts of the said "Assemblies," for opening and extending the navigation of Potomac River, it is provided and enacted, "That in case the said company should not begin the work mentioned in the said Act, within one year after the company should be formed; or if the navigation should not be made and improved between the *Great Falls* and *Fort Cumberland*, in the manner hereinbefore mentioned, within three years after the said company should be formed, then the said company should not be entitled to any benefit, privilege, or advantage, under the said Act."

That your petitioners conceive the intention of the Legislatures in limiting the company to three years, after its formation, for making and improving the navigation between the Great Falls and Fort Cumberland, was to prevent any unnecessary delay in executing the work, and on the presumption that the time allowed was fully sufficient to effect it in the common and usual course of the seasons.

That the said company have entered on the work, within the time limited, and prosecuted the same, at great expense, with unremitted assiduity, with such prospect of success, that they hope and expect to complete the whole navigation within the ten years allowed; but that the latter part of the summer, and the fall of 1785, were so unfavorable, that the hands employed in the bed of the river, above the *Great Falls*, were often drove from their work by the rises of the water, and frequently kept out for several days together, so that the work could not proceed as was wished and expected. And the last summer hath proved so very rainy, that the water has constantly kept up too high to permit any work to be done in the bed of the river; though the company retained a considerable number of men in their service through the whole of the last winter, with the view of being prepared to enter on the work with great force, about the 20th of June, the time that the water is commonly low enough for such purpose; and thus, by extraordinary exertion, to retrieve the unavoidable loss of time in the preceding year.

Your petitioners, therefore, on behalf of the said company, pray that acts of the said Assemblies may be passed whereby the said company may be indulged with time till the seventeenth day of November, 1790, or such other time as to your Honors shall seem reasonable for making and improving the navigation between the Great Falls and Fort Cumberland.

And your petitioners, &c.

In behalf of the Board,

Signed, G. WASHINGTON,

President.

www.ingramcontent.com/pod-product-compliance
Lightning Source LLC
LaVergne TN
LVHW011233110826
845150LV00006B/1626

9781425514143